Glorious Greetings

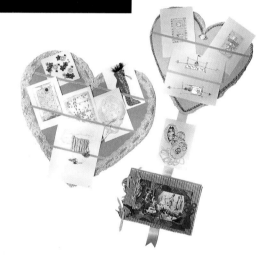

Glorious Greetings
Kate Twelvetrees

Chilton Book Company
Radnor, Pennsylvania

Contents

Collage and Relief

Printing and Painting

A QUARTO BOOK

Copyright © 1996 Quarto Inc.

ISBN 0-8019-8760-1

A CIP record for this book is available from the Library of Congress.

First published in the United States by Chilton Book Company, Radnor, Pennsylvania.

This book was designed and produced by Quarto Inc.
The Old Brewery
6 Blundell Street
London N7 9BH

Senior Editor Anna Selby
Editors Diana Craig, Carolyn Pyrah
Senior Art Editor Clare Baggaley
Designers Debbie Mole, Rowan Seymour, Sheila Volpe
Photographers Laura Wickenden, Paul Forrester, Colin Bowling
Principal Illustrator Vana Haggerty
Illustrator Neil Ballpit
Art Director Moira Clinch
Editorial Director Mark Dartford

Papercraft

Fanciful Fabric

Labor of Love

Typeset in Great Britain by
Central Southern Typesetters,
Eastbourne
Manufactured in Hong Kong by
Regent Publishing Services Ltd
Printed in China by
Leefung-Asco Printers Ltd

Publisher's Note
The author and publishers have made every effort to ensure that all instructions given in this book are safe and accurate, but they cannot accept liability for any resulting injury, loss or damage to either property or person whether direct or consequential and howsoever arising.

Introduction

CELEBRATING THE CHANGES of the seasons, the festivals which punctuate our year, and significant personal events are an important part of our lives. The rise in popularity of purchased handmade cards reflects our desire to mark these occasions in a special way. Making our own handmade greetings echoes a time before mass-produced cards were available when every greeting was handmade. The time, love, and work which went into these "keepsake cards" meant that they were treasured – kept in a memento box, inside a book or album, or even framed.

This book offers several approaches to making handmade cards. There are step-by-step instructions describing many different craft techniques in detail, and suggestions of ways in which to use the many different craft tools and kits available. Through these you will be able to experiment with a wide variety of techniques, even if you have no experience of crafts. There are also cards which use other skills, such as dressmaking and embroidery, to make images for cards; and there are many examples of cards which may inspire you to approach card making in the way I do – collecting all kinds of materials and objects from different sources and combining them to make collages. This open-ended approach needs few tools or formal techniques.

It's easy to begin to make your own professional handmade cards. Many people have always made their own Christmas cards. You only need a small amount of space and a few essential pieces of equipment – and you can often adapt what you have. Card making is inexpensive, and because you are working on such a small scale, it is possible to

use the best materials which would generally be too costly. I use one exquisite hand-embroidered fabric which costs more than $100 a yard, but a tiny amount makes many cards.

Making your own cards has the added advantage that you can easily give the card a personal significance for the person receiving it – incorporating names, favorite objects and colors, relevant themes, messages, and photographs. You will find many examples of ways to do this in this book. Making cards is also a perfect activity to do with children of all ages: it is a means by which they can create an expressive gift for family or friends – they are certainly likely to enjoy it, and the results will be cherished. My children, aged three and eight, often come into my studio, gather up little pieces of materials and a card, and combine these with bits and pieces they have collected in the woods and park to make their own beautifully designed cards.

Look for inspiration for your cards in the gallery sections, which show commercial handmade cards using an astonishing variety of techniques and materials. Use the book as you might use a recipe book, adapting the lists of materials to what you have available. Think back to other techniques you may have used as a child, or use now in other areas of your life, such as plaiting, knotting, and even such activities as cooking and carpentry. Look in libraries for books on traditional craft techniques and adapt them to use in your cards. Experiment and play – above all, have fun.

Collecting materials

Once you begin to look around you for materials for your cards, you will see possibilities everywhere. Collect everything you can and store things in little boxes or envelopes until you think of ways in which to use them. Or play with different materials on a card and see what images occur. This is an exciting way of working, and anything is possible.

● **From nature** The beach, countryside, city parks, and gardens.
Shells, feathers, pebbles, seeds, leaves, flowers (pressed, dried or fresh), driftwood.

● **Libraries**
Look for out-of-copyright prints and texts.

● **Around the home**
Pasta, nuts and seeds, dried chilies, aluminum foil, string, wire, buttons, scraps of fabric, upholstery trimmings, broken jewelry, wrapping paper, used stamps.

● **For general supplies**
Craft stores, art-material
suppliers and printmakers
sell artists' paper, paints,
tools, and equipment,
including new and specialist
products. Notions counters
sell a wide variety of
ribbons, trimmings, fabrics,
and buttons.

● **Unusual/unexpected
shops**
Jewelry findings, theatrical
suppliers, hardware stores,
thrift shops and flea
markets, florists, stationery
stores, candy stores.

● **Recycled materials**
Soft-drink cans, wooden
soft-cheese boxes,
packaging of all kinds.

● **Ephemera** Your own or
from fairs or markets.
Old envelopes, letters,
documents, and postcards.

Basic Equipment

You will only need a few general pieces of equipment. Each card in the book uses a particular craft technique and the tools you will need for that individual card will be specified in the Materials list.

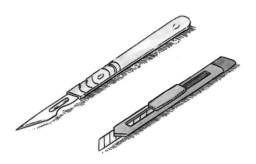

● A **cutting mat**
A piece of cardboard is adequate for most purposes, although, unlike a cutting mat, it retains score marks from a knife and so you will need to change it quite frequently for accuracy.

● A good **craft knife**
This is essential – always cut away from your body and with great care. Many professionals use a scalpel instead. However, scalpels are extremely sharp, and the greatest care must be taken when using them.

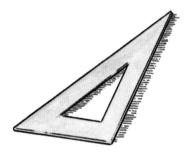

● Sharp **scissors**
Keep the scissors you use for fabric separate from paper or other scissors.

● A **carpenter's square**
Especially helpful for cutting accurate right angles. A paper guillotine is also useful, but not essential.

● A metal **ruler**

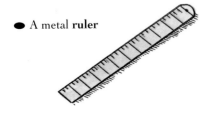

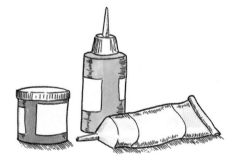

● **Glue**
Three types of glue should cover all your requirements. You will find a reputable fabric/paper glue the most useful. A strong all-purpose glue will join most other materials, and white or yellow craft glue dries transparent.

● **Brushes**
Inexpensive artist's brushes in small, medium, and large size are adequate for most purposes, unless a card requires a more specialist brush.

● **Iron-on adhesive**
This can be used to stick both paper and fabric.

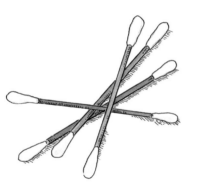

● **Needles and thread**

● **Cotton swabs**
Very useful for applying glue.

● **Tape**
Cellophane tape, masking tape, doubled-sided tape, and magic tape are all useful.

Safety First

Polymer clays (fimo) give off noxious fumes. Always work in a well-ventilated room, and as an additional precaution, do not leave children or pets (including birds) in the kitchen while you are baking clay. The plasticizer in unbaked clays leaches out, so do not use utensils and containers that you use for food preparation for storing or working with clay. As an added precaution, do not use articles made of clay, even when it has been baked, to store or serve food. Always wash your hands thoroughly after you have been working with polymer clay.

~

When cutting sheet metal or wire, such as copper or aluminum, protect your eyes and hands, and file all edges smooth.

Basic Techniques

The difference between a professional looking handmade card and one which just looks homemade is simply the application of a few simple rules. Practicing these techniques will be worthwhile.

Making a Card
~

You can buy ready-made cards, with or without windows, but it is very straightforward to make your own.

Cutting and scoring a plain card

1 Use medium-weight cardboard or thick paper, such as watercolor paper. You can deckle-edge the paper – see opposite. Cut the board with a craft knife and straightedge to the height you desire and double the width. Use a square and ruler to insure the corners are square, and always work on a cutting mat or a piece of thick cardboard.

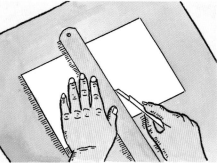

2 Mark the center line of the card on the outside of the board with a pencil and lightly score this line with a craft knife, taking care to mark only the top layer of the board or paper with the knife. After completing your card – it is easier to work with the card open and flat – fold the board along the score mark.

Cutting a window

1 Using a square, mark the shape of your window on the card with a pencil. Use a ruler to measure from the edge of the card to check that the window is centered correctly and is not crooked.

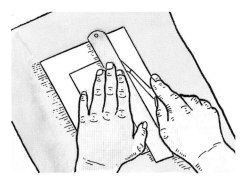

2 Carefully cut out the window using a craft knife and ruler. Be careful not to extend the cuts beyond the corners of the card. Cut the window by working into and away from the corners for accuracy.

Tracing and transferring an image

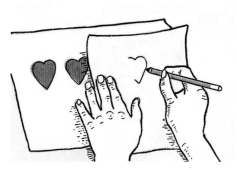

Use tracing or thin layout paper to trace the lines of the picture you wish to transfer. Turn the tracing over and scribble all over the back of the image with a pencil. Turn the tracing right side up and lay the picture on the card. Holding the image steady with one hand, go over the lines of the drawing again with a pencil to transfer to your card.

Masking an image

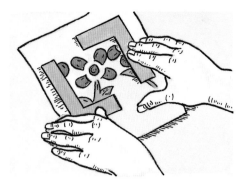

Cut two L-shaped pieces of cardboard, using a carpenter's square so that the corners are accurate. Use these to choose the area of a larger print or picture which you would like to frame. By laying them on the picture surface and moving them, you can frame any size and shape of picture. When you are satisfied, mark the area chosen at the corners with a pencil mark and use a ruler and craft knife to cut the shape – don't forget to add a border to fit under a frame if necessary.

Tearing a deckle edge

The torn edge which you sometimes find on watercolor and handmade paper is very attractive. Mark your line with a pencil mark at both margins. Fold the paper over sharply along this line. Use a ruler or kitchen knife pulled through the fold to tear the paper. Do this a little at a time while holding the paper firmly to avoid ripping the paper.

Antiquing paper

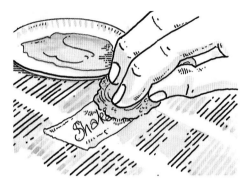

Brush diluted instant coffee over a photocopy of a print. Use a large brush or a sponge and test for color on a spare piece of paper first as it will dry a darker shade. Don't worry about water marks and different patches of color, as this will give a better effect. When dry, cut or tear out the pieces you require. If tearing, tear the picture area toward you and away from the background: this will give a stained, rather than a white, edge.

Mounting a print

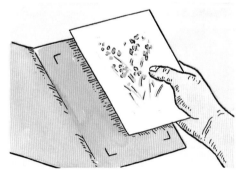

Check that the print is square to the card by measuring from the edges (the border). Mark the corners with pencil, so that you can quickly register the glued print.

Basic Guidelines

These are apparently simple rules, but it is worth becoming a perfectionist as they can make a dramatic difference to your results. You are not aiming for the uniform look of a mass-produced card, but you do want one which looks crafted and professional.

● Always use a knife with a sharp blade, and if you want a straight line, use a ruler and a good, smooth cutting surface. If you want a right angle, use a carpenter's square.

● Make sure windows are cut square to your backing and always mount images square to their background, unless you are aiming for a deliberately asymmetrical effect.

● Always use a craft knife rather than scissors, when appropriate.

● It is important to use good-quality materials, including cardboard of sufficient weight to support the image – this often lets a card down.

● Make sure the score mark is parallel to the mount edges, or the card will not fold properly.

● Never let glue be seen on your pictures.

● Always practice new techniques on spare paper first.

Basic Stitches
~

A number of the cards in this book use stitches as part of their technique. These include sewing stitches, as well as some simple embroidery stitches.

Slip stitch

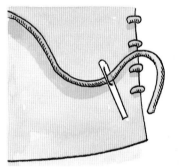

Slipstitches form a neat line of small plain stitches. Bring the thread through to the right side. Insert the needle again to make a stitch and bring it through farther along. Continue in this way to form a line of small stitches.

Stab stitch

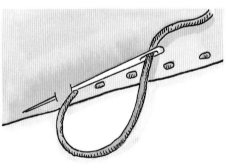

This uses the same technique to make a tiny stitch which is almost invisible on the right side. Stab the needle through the material immediately after the place where you brought the thread up on the right side. Leave a longer gap before bringing the needle through for the next stitch.

Back stitch

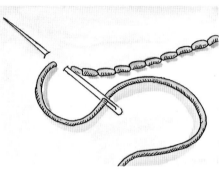

Start with an ordinary stitch and then take the needle back to the end of the previous stitch. Take the point of the needle through to the reverse and bring it through to the right side one stitch ahead. Pull the thread through, then take another backward stitch and proceed in the same way to form a line of joined stitches.

Stem stitch

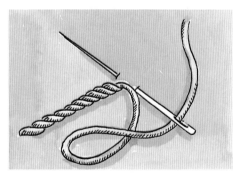

If you are right-handed, work from left to right taking small, equal backstitches with the needle inserted from right to left. Keep the thread to the right of the needle. The needle is at a slight angle so that the back stitches overlap slightly as you work. This stitch is often used for flower stems and outlines.

Blanket stitch

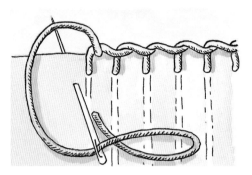

This is worked along the edge of a piece of material. Insert the needle below the edge of the material to the reverse side and so that the needle shows beyond the edge of the material. Loop the thread under the needle and pull it through with the thread below the needle. Space the stitches apart to form a rolled edge.

French knots

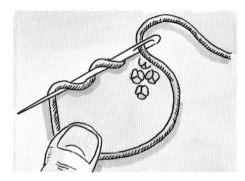

Pull the thread through where you would like to make the French knot. Hold the thread down with the opposite hand and wind the thread twice around the needle.

Tighten the knots and pull the needle back to insert it at the starting point and pull the needle through.

Overstitch on the reverse side to secure, or work another stitch.

Daisy stitch

Commonly used to make leaf and flower shapes, daisy stitch is an isolated chain stitch. Start with a knot on the reverse side and bring the thread through and hold it down with the thumb of your opposite hand.

Reinsert the needle close to where the thread came out, and bring the point out a short distance away so that the thread you are holding loops under the needle point. Pull the thread through gently and fasten the top of the loop with a tiny anchoring stitch.

Gift Wrapping

Wrap your card as you would any gift to make it even more special. Remember to pack and pad your card carefully if you are mailing it, to avoid damage.

Box

~

METHOD

1 Measure the length and width of your cardboard, add ½ inch, and make this your base size, using the template below.

2 Cut out the shape using a craft knife and ruler. Score along fold lines. Apply glue to the front side of the flaps which are shaded in the diagram, and assemble the box, flaps inside.

3 You can cover the box with fabric or patterned paper cut to the same size and stuck in place with iron-on adhesive or fabric/paper glue. Cover the box while flat, before gluing the flaps.

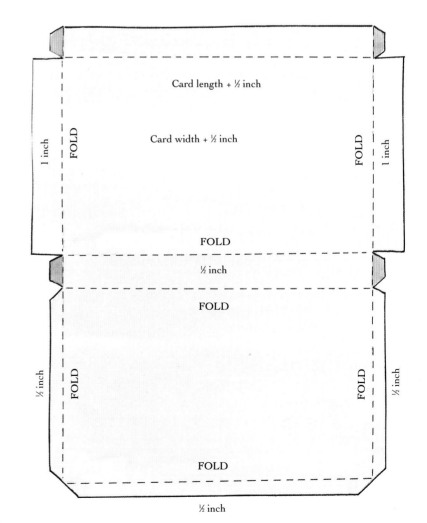

Card length + ½ inch

Card width + ½ inch

1 inch   FOLD   FOLD   1 inch

FOLD

½ inch

FOLD

½ inch   FOLD   FOLD   ½ inch

FOLD

½ inch

Envelope

~

METHOD

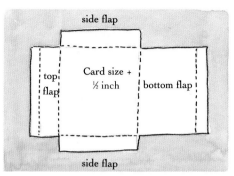

1 Plan the size of paper required to make the envelope. The basic rectangle should be slightly bigger than the card size. Add a bottom flap three-quarters of the basic width plus ½ inch. Add a top flap a quarter of the basic width plus ½ inch. Make 1¼-inch side flaps.

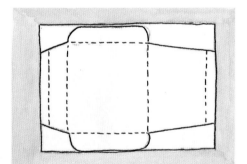

2 Draw the basic shape on the paper. (You can add lining paper using colored or tissue paper the width and length of the envelope minus the bottom flap. Glue it in place before you assemble the envelope.) For a professional finish, use a coin to draw curves on the side flaps. Gently taper the top and bottom flaps.

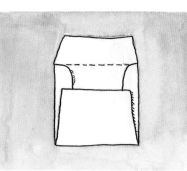

3 Fold in the side flaps, then glue the edges of the bottom flap, turn this up, and stick it to the side flaps. Neatly fold over the top flap, then lift it up again and stick double-sided tape below the edge to make a seal.

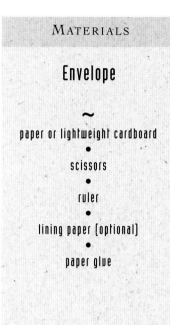

MATERIALS

Envelope

~

paper or lightweight cardboard

•

scissors

•

ruler

•

lining paper (optional)

•

paper glue

Wrapping Ideas

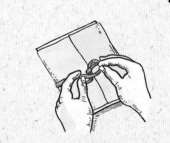

● Wrap with tissue paper and tie with ribbon.

● Buy a card box from a craft store and cover it with pretty decorative paper.

● Make a box using textured or patterned cardboard (see opposite).

● Look for envelopes made from handmade papers in art supply stores and good stationery stores and make cards to fit them.

● Seal your envelopes with sealing wax and one of the beautiful decorative seals available.

● Make your own envelope using watercolor or textured paper, perhaps with deckle edging (see page 13).

● Decorate the wrapping paper with rubber stamps, stencils, or even shells and charms threaded on your ribbon. The wrapping can reflect the card inside.

Introduction

While it appears to be one of the simplest of techniques — that of arranging different collected elements into a design — collage/assemblage/relief can be one of the most fascinating and varied methods for card-making. Anything is possible — look around you and you will see possible materials in almost every situation. (We've included lots of suggestions for making a collection on pages 8—9.) The keys to successful collage-making are simplicity, an eye for balance, and the relationship between materials and colors. Experiment with combinations of paper, fabric, and objects against your background. Don't be afraid to keep changing things around — although the first spontaneous arrangement may be the

Collage and Relief

best. Sometimes I have seen the idea for a card in the accidental juxtaposition of materials on my worktable. Reduce or add until you achieve harmony and balance. Looking at your picture in a mirror can help — the reversed image gives you a fresh view. The small framework within which you are working means that a fraction of an inch can make a huge difference, but this is a technique to learn like any other and as you "play," your eye will develop.

Fall Leaves
~

This card is made from a very strong, textured watercolor board, and was purchased with a torn deckle edge on one side. It has been cut and scored so that the back of the card is wider than the front, showing the deckle edge. This gives the card a more interesting, layered look when it is closed. Press leaves for the card in a heavy book, between sheets of blotting paper or smooth tissues, and leave at least one month, until they are dry and papery.

MATERIALS

Fall Leaves
~

watercolor board, 8¼ × 15 inches, chosen and scored to fold as described above

•

straw paper or other textured paper, same size as front of folded card

•

8 × 10 typing paper

•

newspaper

•

1 large leaf, such as a fern, either fresh or pressed

•

selection of leaves, pressed

•

gold acrylic paint

•

rust-red acrylic paint

•

small brush

•

old toothbrush

•

craft knife

•

cutting mat

•

paper glue

•

craft glue

METHOD

1 Cover the work surface with newspaper. Squeeze some rust-red paint onto a plate. Lay the fern leaf on the *outside back* of the card. Mask most of the front of the card with a piece of paper, except for a strip near the score mark; the card should be open, flat on the work surface. Dip the toothbrush into the paint.

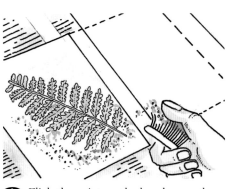

2 Flick the paint on the brush over the leaf with your finger. Do this until all the spaces between the parts of the leaf are spattered with paint.

3 Don't be tempted to lift the leaf to look, because you won't be able to get the leaf in exactly the same place again. When you have finished, lift the leaf up very carefully and allow the paint to dry.

4 Cut a rectangle from straw paper slightly smaller than the front of the card. Roughly tear this down the left-hand edge, so that this edge falls just short of the spatter marks which will have overlapped onto the front of the card. Arrange leaves in a falling pattern on the paper, and when you are satisfied with the design, lift them, one by one, and glue them, taking great care not to break the brittle leaves.

5 Highlight some, but not all, of the leaves by dabbing on gold acrylic paint.

6 Apply a thin layer of paper glue to the back of the straw paper and quickly glue it to the card. Glue one small leaf with craft glue on the back of the card in the bottom left-hand corner.

Variation
Use a sponge instead of a toothbrush, and press it over the leaf, or mix the two techniques, using two or three leaves and different paint colors.

front

back

Christmas Tree Presents

~

*The images on this flat card have been made
from a fine webbing used by dressmakers.*

METHOD

1 Paint pieces of the vilene with gold and green fabric paint and allow to dry.

2 Make miniature presents by folding the scraps of blue cardboard into squares and tying them with thread.

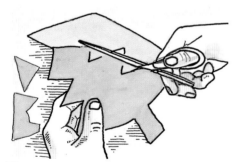

3 Cut a rectangle of gold vilene and a tree shape of green vilene, and glue these in place on the card.

4 Tear strips of blue paper and glue to the edges of the card. Cut out a blue paper pot to hold the tree, and glue in place.

5 Decorate with glitter by applying glue, sprinkling with glitter, and shaking off excess. Glue on the presents and sequins.

Christmas Tree

~

*The polymer clay relief combines well with the
printed background. Painted modeling clay
could be used as an alternative. An old teaspoon
was used to make the indentations.*

METHOD

1 Roll out the polymer clay. Cut out the tree in green and the pot in brown. Press foliage patterns into the tree, and ridges into pot with the modeling tools. Bake the clay according to the manufacturer's directions.

2 Fill in the patterns on the tree and pot with glitter glue.

3 Cut a potato in half and then cut a star shape in the flat side by marking the star with a craft knife and then cutting away the potato around it. Press this shape into fairly thick paint, and use it to print a pattern on the front of the card.

4 Cut a frame to fit the front of the card from the colored paper or cardboard. Glue in place.

5 Glue the Christmas tree and pot to the front of the card.

MATERIALS

Christmas Tree Presents

~

pale pink plain card, 6¼ × 6¼ inches
•
blue paper for border and scraps of different blue for presents
•
vilene (a stiffening material for dressmaking)
•
gold sequins
•
paintbrush
•
gold and silver thread
•
green and gold fabric paint
•
gold and silver glitter
•
craft knife
•
cutting mat
•
fabric/paper glue

Christmas Tree

~

plain card, 6 × 8¼ inches, scored to fold in middle
•
thick paper or thin cardboard in a contrasting color
•
green and brown polymer clay or modeling clay and paints (see page 11)
•
acrylic or poster paint
•
glitter glue
•
potato
•
modeling tools
•
craft knife
•
cutting mat
•
craft glue

Papier-Mâché Initial
~

You could choose the favorite colors of the recipient for the initial on this card. The card is spattered with matching and coordinating colors.

MATERIALS

Papier-Mâché Initial
~

plain blue card, 5¼ × 8¼ inches, scored to fold in middle

•

corrugated cardboard

•

thin paper or tissue

•

black, white, and choice of acrylic paints

•

wallpaper paste

•

paintbrush

•

old toothbrush

•

brooch finding and all-purpose glue (optional)

•

scissors

•

cutting mat

•

craft glue

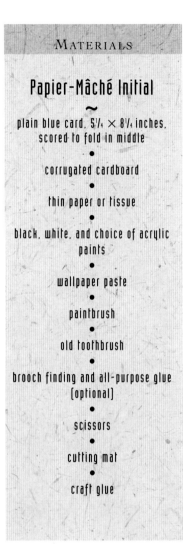

METHOD

1 Cut the shape of the initial from corrugated cardboard.

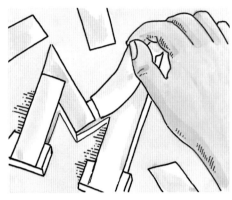

2 Cover with strips of thin paper or tissue, brushed with wallpaper paste. Do about three layers, and allow each layer to dry before adding the next.

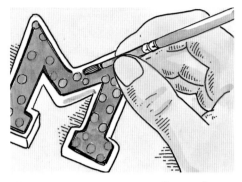

3 When dry, paint white, allow to dry again, then paint a pattern on the letter.

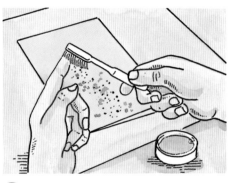

4 Spatter the front of the card with paint: apply quite dry paint to a toothbrush and run your finger over the brush, flicking the paint onto the surface.

5 Glue the letter to the card, or glue a brooch finding to the back of the initial with strong glue and pin to the card. Self-adhesive brooch pins are also available.

Safety warning
Wear gloves and do not inhale while using wallpaper paste. Try instead to get a nonfungicide craft product, specially for papier-mâché, available at craft stores.

Variation
If you have the time, make all the letters of the name. Don't mount them, but make holes through the tops of the letters and string them together.

Floral Brooch
~

This clay takes two days to dry. For a quicker result, use polymer clay (see page 11).

METHOD

1 Cut off a section of clay. Roll or pat flat until it is about ⅛ inch thick and measures 3 × 3 inches. Draw the outline of flowers and vase by scoring the clay lightly.

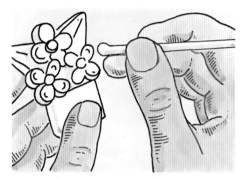

2 Carefully cut out the brooch shape with a clay tool. Make the markings on the flowers and leaves with a molding tool. Roll three small balls for flower centers and press them flat. Dampen the centers of the flowers gently and press them on.

3 Smooth the whole brooch surface with a medium-sized brush or fingers dipped in water, and allow to dry for about two days.

4 When dry, smooth with fine sandpaper, then paint using the fine paintbrush. When the paint is dry, varnish front and back. Glue on the brooch finding.

5 Cut out one contrasting piece of cardboard and draw a grid of ¼-inch squares for the tablecloth. Cut out the shape of the curtains, glue to the tablecloth, then glue both to the card and add details with the other colored cardboard.

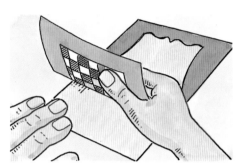

6 Place the finished brooch on the card and anchor it with a loop of wire passed through the brooch pin and twisted inside the card. On the front of the card, align the brooch with a small piece of handy-tack.

Variation
Personalize this professional-looking brooch to suit the recipient(s). You could paint a number 50 in gold for a wedding anniversary, make a pet owner's cat, or some vegetables for a gardener.

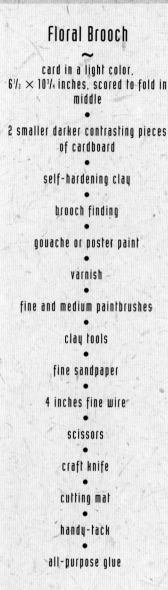

MATERIALS

Floral Brooch
~

card in a light color, 6½ × 10¾ inches, scored to fold in middle

•

2 smaller darker contrasting pieces of cardboard

•

self-hardening clay

•

brooch finding

•

gouache or poster paint

•

varnish

•

fine and medium paintbrushes

•

clay tools

•

fine sandpaper

•

4 inches fine wire

•

scissors

•

craft knife

•

cutting mat

•

handy-tack

•

all-purpose glue

"Wear me" Bracelet

~

The delicate pastel colors of this card give it a very special quality, and it's fun at the same time because the bracelet can be removed and worn.

METHOD

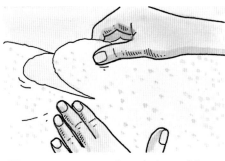

1 Tear out an egg-shaped piece of the decorative paper and wrap a piece of organza ribbon around its base to make a basket, gluing the ends of the ribbon to the back of the paper. Glue the paper to the card.

2 With a pin, make two pairs of small holes through the card at the top of the egg-shaped paper. Thread two short lengths of wire through these from the inside of the card, make tight loops over the bracelet to suspend it on the card, and thread the wire back inside the card. Secure by twisting the wire.

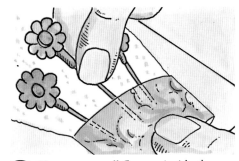

3 Glue some small flowers inside the ribbon basket.

4 You can also write "wear me" on a small scrap of backing paper and glue it to the bottom of the card.

Variation
This also makes a good Easter card. Omit the bracelet, and cut out small pictures of eggs, chicks, etc. Glue these to the backing paper above the basket. Alternately, make a bracelet from elastic and small wooden alphabet beads, saying "happy birthday" or "good luck."

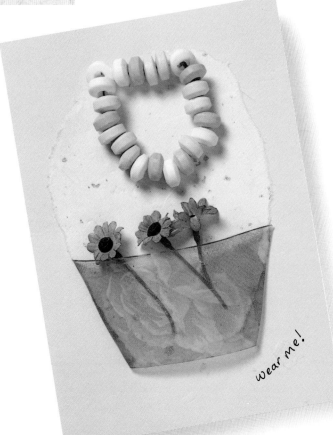

Rose Nest

~

Dried roses are evocative of summer days, parties, wedding bouquets . . . This rose is tucked into a fluffy pink nest of wool.

METHOD

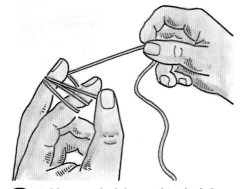

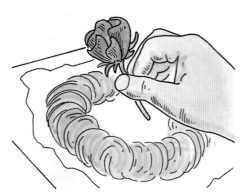

Rose Nest

~

plain ivory or cream card,
6 × 8¼ inches, scored to fold in middle

•

small piece of white tissue paper

•

dried rose with short stem

•

angora-style fluffy wool,
approximately 3 yards long

•

fabric/paper glue

1 Hold one end of the wool in the left hand and, with fingers slightly apart, wind the wool loosely around them about 14 times. Remove from fingers and push half of the woolen skein through the hole in the center to achieve a twisted effect and to stop the wool from unraveling. Wrap the end of the wool under and over the ring of wool a few times.

4 Glue the dried rose in the center, tucking the stem under the wool for extra support. As dried roses are particularly fragile, dot small amounts of glue between the petals on the side of the rose which is being glued to the card.

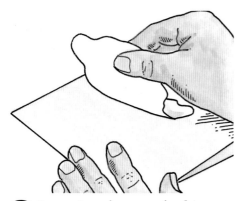

2 Tear an irregular rectangle of tissue paper, and glue it to the front of the card.

3 Glue the woolen "nest" to the card, making sure that both ends are firmly attached, and that there is no glue on the front of the nest.

Birthday Candles
~

This makes a pretty, tactile card for a child's birthday. Alternately, for a more sophisticated version to send to an adult, follow the instructions in the variation, below.

Birthday Candles
~

plain card, 6 × 8¼ inches, scored to fold in middle

•

nursery-patterned ribbon

•

birthday candles (number as child's age)

•

silk flowers

•

scissors

•

fabric/paper glue

•

all-purpose glue

METHOD

1 Cut strips of ribbon to fit around the sides of the card and glue in place: apply a thin layer of fabric glue to the card, rather than the ribbon, so that it does not stain the ribbon. Glue the bottom ribbon at the ends and bottom edge, to form a pocket.

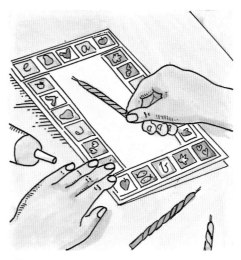

2 Glue the candles to the card with thin lines of all-purpose glue.

3 Put a little craft glue on the back of the flower stems and tuck inside the ribbon pocket, covering base of candles.

Variation

For a more sophisticated card, simply substitute the nursery ribbon with velvet or lace. Seasonal cards can be made with appropriate silk flowers.

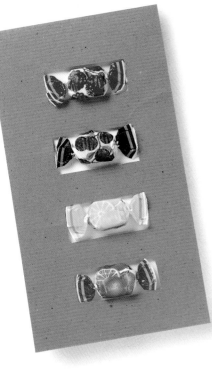

Candy in the Windows
~

Many candies have pretty wrappers suitable for making collages. In this case, whole candies with their wrappers have been glued to the card.

METHOD

1 Cover the front and back of the card with brown paper cut to fit: apply a thin layer of paper glue to the card and press the brown paper on quickly, smoothing it out toward the sides. (The paper looks best flat side out.)

2 Place the candy on the front of the card and draw box shapes around them. Open the card out and cut these windows out carefully with a sharp craft knife.

3 Close the card and use all-purpose glue to attach the candy to the inside of the card through their windows to make sure that they are in the right place.

Variation
For a child's card, make a face with candy. Cut out a face-shaped window, and attach two round candies for the eyes, and a rectangular or oval one for the mouth.

River Fish
~

Create interesting effects by photocopying drawings, prints, etc. on clear acetate and layering other papers or fabric behind. The fish-eye rivets hold the acetate to the card.

METHOD

1 Make a drawing, or use cutout prints of fish, and arrange and glue the images on to white paper. Photocopy them on acetate, reducing or enlarging if necessary.

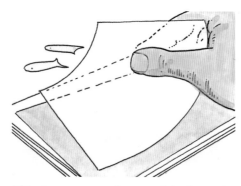

2 Cut acetate to the size of the front of the card and cut the blue paper and tissue paper into interesting background shapes and layer them on the card. Hold the acetate on top to check the position. Cut two fish shapes from gold cardboard.

3 Put the two gold fish behind the acetate in two corners of the mount, reposition the acetate, and anchor all the layers together using the rivet gun, with the rivets as fish eyes.

MATERIALS

Candy in the Windows
~

plain card, 5 × 18 inches, scored to fold in the middle

•

brown wrapping paper

•

4 pieces of wrapped candy

•

scissors and craft knife

•

cutting mat

•

fabric/paper glue

•

all-purpose glue

River Fish
~

plain card, 6 × 8¼ inches, scored to fold in middle

•

8 × 10 sheet typing paper

•

shiny blue paper

•

wave-patterned tissue paper

•

small pieces of gold cardboard

•

acetate film, 8 × 10 inches

•

black and white drawing or print

•

rivets and rivet gun

•

scissors or craft knife

•

cutting mat

•

paper glue

Woven Initial

~

You can use all sorts of natural objects for this card – small shells or pebbles, tiny pieces of glass smoothed by the sea, seeds, or even pressed leaves or flower heads. Wood veneer is available from woodwork suppliers.

MATERIALS

Woven Initial

~

thick, stiff watercolor paper with torn deckle edge, 8¾ × 15 inches, scored to fold in middle

•

dark blue background paper, slightly smaller than mount

•

sheet of wood veneer, 4 × 8 inches

•

rope or cord, 35 inches long

•

turquoise acrylic paint

•

pebble

•

cotton ball

•

scissors

•

cutting mat

•

all-purpose glue

METHOD

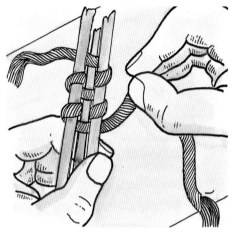

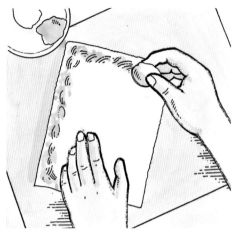

1 Gently break off six narrow strips of wood veneer to make the initial. Hold three strips in one hand and weave the rope or cord through them, weaving the thread back along the next part of the letter with the same piece. If the length of rope runs out halfway through, just leave an extra piece hanging.

2 Dab paint around the edges of the card, using cotton ball. Use quite wet paint the first time and then repeat with very dry paint for an illusion of depth.

3 Glue the dark blue paper to the card and then carefully glue on the initial, making sure that no glue gets onto the front. Glue an extra strip of veneer at the bottom of the initial, to underline it, and add a small pebble to punctuate.

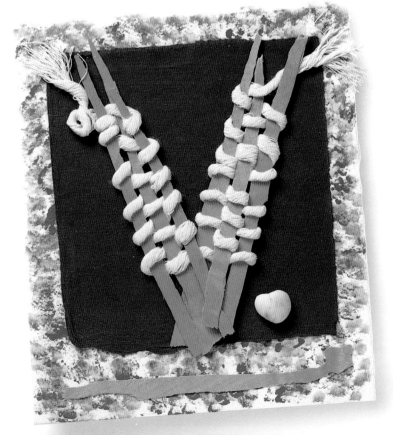

Shells in the Sand

~

It's simple to create your own sand art designs, using double-sided self-adhesive film. Alternately, use one of the many kits available.

METHOD

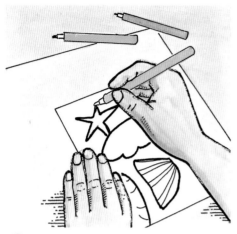

1 Draw your design in color on the paper, keeping it fairly simple – you will be cutting out each area of color.

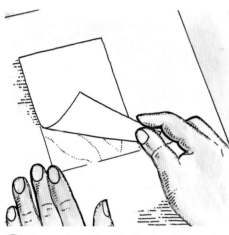

2 Cut a piece of self-adhesive film to the size of your design and transfer your design onto this. Peel the release paper off the back of the film and press the film firmly onto the card.

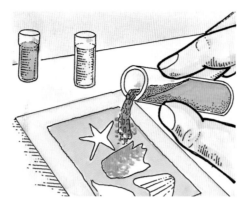

3 Cut around each area of color in your picture with a craft knife, taking care to cut only through the release paper and not through the film itself. Peel off the darkest area of the design and sprinkle the colored sand onto this, shaking off excess. Proceed in the same way for each area of the design: you can create interesting effects by mixing the sand colors before sprinkling them on, or by sprinkling one color very lightly on the film and a little of another on top.

4 Glue some real shells to the finished sand picture.

MATERIALS

Shells in the Sand

~

plain card, 6 × 8¼ inches, scored to fold in middle

•

sheet of 8 × 10 typing paper

•

double-sided self-adhesive film

•

fine sand in a variety of colors

•

shells

•

colored pencils

•

craft knife

•

cutting mat

•

all-purpose glue

Present Postcard
~

Write a simple message or name with sand and glue on a foreign stamp and shells to evoke pleasant memories of travels abroad.

MATERIALS

Present Postcard
~

plain card, 5¾ × 8¼ inches, scored to fold in middle

•

piece of soft watercolor paper, torn to a postcard shape

•

soft, fine white tissue paper

•

blue sand

•

used postage stamp

•

small shells

•

thin lurex thread

•

craft knife or scissors

•

cutting mat

•

all-purpose glue

METHOD

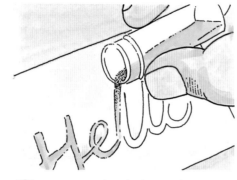

1 Write a word with glue on the postcard-shaped paper: remove the cap directly above where you wish to start writing, as the glue will drip. Quickly and loosely write the word. Sprinkle the sand over the glue, wait a few moments, shake off surplus, and allow to dry.

2 Glue on postage stamp and shells.

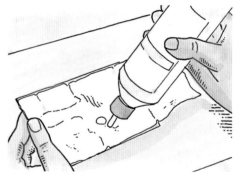

3 Tear strips of tissue paper and wrap them around the top and bottom of the card, covering only parts of the card. Glue the edges behind the card.

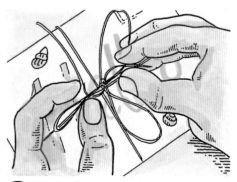

4 Tie the "postcard" with the lurex thread, like a present, with long threads hanging from the central bow. Glue the postcard to the card.

Embossed Key

~

Use the many powders available to emboss the surface of a rubber stamp. This stamp was copied from an eighteenth-century print, but there is a great variety of purchased stamps available. To make your own stamp, see Flying Hearts, page 61.

METHOD

1 Tear a piece of the red paper to fit within the front of the card. Apply embossing ink evenly to the stamp pad, following the manufacturer's directions. Print the key on the paper and sprinkle the print with the embossing powder, shaking off excess.

3 Lightly glue the paper to the card. Glue the ribbon to frame the key, following the instructions given for gluing the ribbon in the Ribbon Frame Card on page 108. Cross the ends of the ribbon at the lower center edge and glue them to the card.

MATERIALS

Embossed Key

~

plain card, 6 × 8¼ inches, scored to fold in middle

•

handmade red paper same size as front of card

•

narrow gold ribbon

•

embossing ink and stamp pad

•

silver embossing powder

•

key rubber stamp

•

scissors

•

fabric/paper glue

•

heat gun or toaster

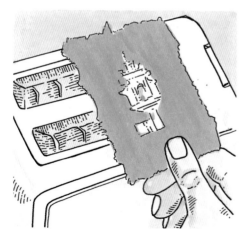

2 Hold the printed paper over a heat source, such as a toaster, or use a heat gun to emboss the image. Again, follow the manufacturer's instructions and take care not to brown the paper.

Gallery

7 Lunchtime Pig

Sparkle Designs
A witty mixed-media collage using paper with miniature toys.

8 Herb Pots

Personal Stamp Exchange
Five layers of card raise a stamped and embossed image of herbs.

9 Silver Cow

Sophie Williams
A tinfoil cow is machine stitched onto an ink-stained and collaged paper background.

10 Food Collages

Tushar Parekh
Two more variations on food collages (see page 37), using glued-on, varnished seeds and chili wrapped in fine wire.

11 Red Sails

Personal Stamp Exchange
Hand-torn tissue paper on a deckle-edged card forms the background for a detailed embossed rubber-stamp image.

12 Sailing in Brittany

Crescent Cardboard Co.
A more complex and very delicately colored version of the sand art technique on page 29.

13 Heart in Heart

Irene Brown
A heart made with twisted copper wire frames a cut-out red heart and overlays printed paper and torn tissue paper.

14 Ceramic Heart

Mary Fellows
A hand-painted and varnished ceramic heart is mounted on two layers of cardboard.

15 Wedding Card

Alana Pryce
This unusual wedding card uses an interesting mixture of gold-painted card and lace with a printed definition of the word "marry."

16 Valentine Hearts

Personal Stamp Exchange
Layers of embossed and painted stamped hearts are tied onto cards with cord or raffia.

Embossed Metal Flower
~

Embossed Metal Flower
~

5³/₄ × 9¹/₂-inch plain card,
scored to fold in middle

•

inner card, cut slightly smaller
than outer card

•

aluminum sheet

•

sequins

•

thin silver wire

•

pin

•

used ballpoint pen, or similar
embossing tool

•

scissors

•

metal file

•

cutting mat

•

tape

•

craft glue

Aluminum sheet is available by the yard from some craft stores. Alternately, you could use an aluminum soda can, which is thin enough to cut with scissors. Take great care not to cut yourself – the edge of the can is extremely sharp.

METHOD

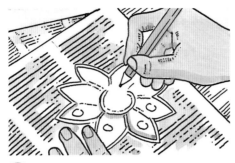

1 Cut your design from the aluminum with scissors and file edges smooth. Place the metal on a fairly soft surface, such as several layers of newspaper, and emboss the reverse side with a used ballpoint pen.

2 Glue the design to the center of the card.

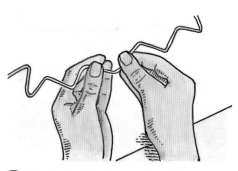

3 Bend the wire into an irregular wavy line – you can do this with your fingers. Using a pin, make two small holes close to each other, near each of the four corners of the card.

4 Push one end of the wavy wire through one of these holes, anchoring it inside the card with tape. Make a border of wire around the card, attaching the wire at each corner with small loops of wire passed through the holes. Twist the wire inside the card to fasten it and then tape it down flat. Finally push the end of the wavy wire through the second small hole and tape down.

5 Glue sequins on the card to decorate. Glue the smaller piece of card over the exposed tape and wire ends on the inside of the card.

String Writing

~

This is an easy way to achieve an embossed metal effect. Have fun experimenting with different thicknesses of string, colored silver paper, and so on.

METHOD

1 Draw the letters of a name on the thin cardboard. Apply craft glue along the outlines and set aside until tacky.

2 Lay the string along the lines of glue and trim the end at the end of each letter. Leave to dry.

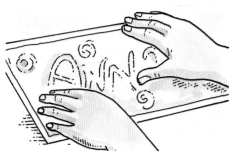

3 Apply craft glue, thinned with water, to the whole surface of the card. Cover the surface of the card with tinfoil and smooth it gently over the string with a cotton ball, allowing the foil to wrinkle. Make sure that the shapes of the letters are clearly visible through it.

4 Brush thinned paint over the foil and, before it dries completely, rub most of it off, leaving just enough to create an "antique" texture. (Practice first on a spare piece of foil.)

5 Glue the picture to the colored paper, and decorate the border with felt-tip pen.

6 Glue the paper to the card.

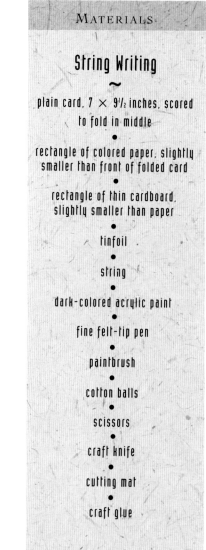

MATERIALS

String Writing

~

plain card, 7 × 9½ inches, scored to fold in middle

•

rectangle of colored paper, slightly smaller than front of folded card

•

rectangle of thin cardboard, slightly smaller than paper

•

tinfoil

•

string

•

dark-colored acrylic paint

•

fine felt-tip pen

•

paintbrush

•

cotton balls

•

scissors

•

craft knife

•

cutting mat

•

craft glue

Stamped Package
~

Use this basic design to make all kinds of personalized cards. There is a wonderful selection of ready-made rubber stamps available, as well as kits to make your own rubber stamps, and specialist stores which will copy any design in perfect detail. Collect used postage stamps so that you can use one relevant to your theme.

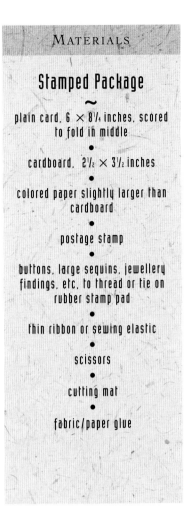

MATERIALS

Stamped Package
~

plain card, 6 × 8¼ inches, scored to fold in middle

•

cardboard, 2½ × 3½ inches

•

colored paper slightly larger than cardboard

•

postage stamp

•

buttons, large sequins, jewellery findings, etc. to thread or tie on rubber stamp pad

•

thin ribbon or sewing elastic

•

scissors

•

cutting mat

•

fabric/paper glue

METHOD

1 Apply glue along the edges of the cardboard and lay it, glue side up, on the colored paper. Fold the edges of the colored paper over the edges and press down to make a "package".

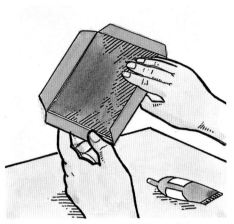

2 Glue a postage stamp to the front of the package, and decorate with rubber stamps. You could write a name or short message in the center.

3 Tie the package with thin ribbon or sewing elastic, threading on buttons or other motifs, and finally glue the parcel to the card.

Variation
Use silver or gold wrapping paper and lurex thread for a Christmas card, decorated with rubber-stamped holly.

Chili Pepper Collage
~

This witty card uses food motifs with beeswax combined in a collage of newspaper and tissue paper.

METHOD

1 Cut the beeswax into a small pleasing shape to fit in one corner of the card. Cut the tissue paper into four rough pieces of different shapes, slightly larger than the beeswax. Cut out a small piece of newspaper around 2½ inches square.

2 Place the cut newspaper at an angle in the center of the card and glue it down with the glue stick.

3 Position layers of tissue paper at different angles over the newspaper and glue each down with the glue stick.

4 When these layers are dry, glue the beeswax into the top left-hand corner of the tissue paper layers with all-purpose clear glue. Position and glue the chili pepper in the same way on the right-hand side of the card.

Busy Bees
~

This card uses specially made bee pins on beeswax. They are available from some craft stores and also there are now stores devoted to "bee products," selling honey, beeswax candles, and bee memorabilia.

METHOD

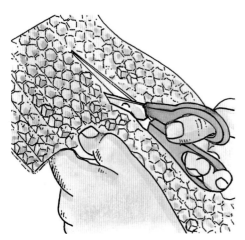

1 Cut out a roughly shaped piece of beeswax to cover the center front of the card, leaving a border all the way around. Position and glue down with all-purpose clear glue.

2 When dry, arrange the bees on the beeswax, then push the pin through the beeswax and the card and secure.

Hand and Heart
~

Make the heart from an old letter or postcard of your own, or look for something suitable in an antique market or manuscript fair. Alternately, you could make your own old "manuscript" from paper artificially aged with coffee and marked with a rubber stamp and some fine handwriting.

METHOD

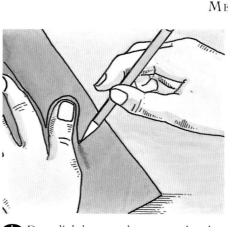

1 Draw lightly around your own hand with a pencil to create a simple outline, then cut it out from the colored paper. Erase any pencil marks.

2 Cut out a heart shape from an old envelope or postcard using the template (see p122), then cut out from red paper a second heart which is approximately ¼ inch larger all around. Glue the envelope or card heart to the red paper heart, then cut a decorative edge around the paper heart by snipping out small triangular shapes.

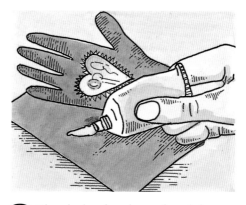

3 Glue the hand to the card, and then glue the heart in the center of the palm of the hand.

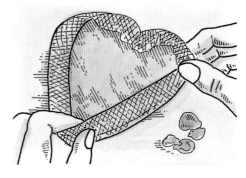

Variation

As an alternative to using a piece of writing, cut the smaller heart from a piece of light-colored, textured paper, place a little potpourri or dried flower petals on top, and cover with a piece of fine net. Fold the net around the edges of the heart, pleating it as necessary, and glue in place behind the heart. Then complete the card as before.

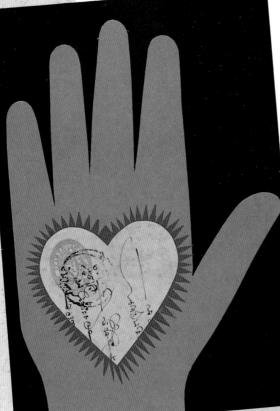

Nostalgic Collage

~

This collage works particularly well because the colors are soft and muted, giving the card an "antique" feel, and the arrangement and careful selection of the objects suggest an old scrapbook or prized collection of ephemera. Press the flowers several weeks in advance (see page 40).

METHOD

1 Cut and tear pieces of old letters, or make your own written fragments using colored ink and paper.

2 Glue the fragments to the card, leaving room around the edges for the border.

3 Cut out a small motif from the lace and glue to the edge along with the pressed flowers. Sew the buttons to the card in the spaces between, using embroidery thread or raffia. Choose one large flower as a focal point and glue in place. Glue on the photocopied motif(s).

Flower Urn

~

Part of the interest of this card lies in the texture of the paper used. Instead of the type of paper shown, you could use one which includes fragments of pressed leaves or flowers. For an unusual addition to this card, glue an envelope of flower seeds inside the card.

METHOD

1 Cut out an urn shape from red paper and glue to the bottom of the card.

2 Cut out small leaf shapes from the green paper and glue them in a tall arch shape above the urn.

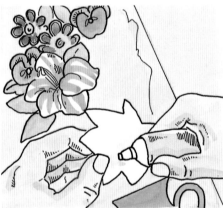

3 Starting at the top of the leaf arch, fill in the space with the cutout flowers and more leaves. Place the smallest flowers at the top to balance the arrangement.

Variation
Try a tall, thin card with a vase of red tulips and long, bright green leaves.

MATERIALS

Nostalgic Collage

~

plain card, 6 × 10¼ inches scored to fold in middle

•

photocopied engravings (stained with coffee for an antiqued effect if desired)

•

old letters

•

pressed flowers

•

scrap of lace

•

small buttons

•

embroidery thread or raffia and needle

•

scissors

•

craft knife

•

cutting mat

•

fabric/paper glue

Flower Urn

~

card made from thick, light-colored textured paper, 10 × 10 inches, scored to fold in middle

•

red paper for urn and green paper for leaves

•

photographs or illustrations of flowers cut from old seed catalogs or gardening magazines

•

craft knife

•

cutting mat

•

paper glue

Pressed Flower Wrap
~

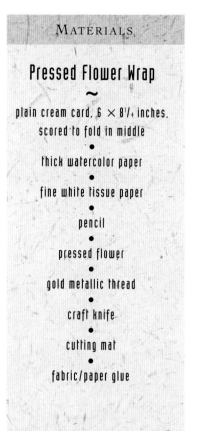

MATERIALS

Pressed Flower Wrap
~

plain cream card, 6 × 8¼ inches,
scored to fold in middle

•

thick watercolor paper

•

fine white tissue paper

•

pencil

•

pressed flower

•

gold metallic thread

•

craft knife

•

cutting mat

•

fabric/paper glue

To press flowers, simply place them in a heavy book, between sheets of blotting paper or smooth tissue paper, and leave for several weeks, then check. Experiment with different flowers, avoiding fleshy ones. The best tissue paper to use for this card is high-quality tissue, available from art-supply stores.

METHOD

1 Lay the flower on the watercolor paper and mark the paper lightly at the edges of the flower with a pencil. Tear out a piece of the paper to fit around the flower.

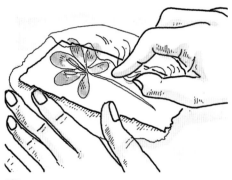

2 Lightly glue the flower to the paper, taking care not to break it.

3 Tear out an irregular piece of tissue paper and wrap it around the flower and paper to form a package or envelope.

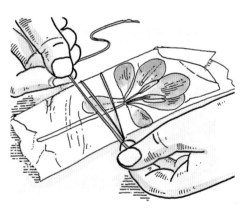

4 Wrap the thread around the package two or three times and knot. Pull the thread between thumb and index finger, in order to corkscrew it.

5 Glue the parcel to the card. Be careful not to get any glue on the tissue paper in front.

Feather Card
~

To copy this card, the feather should not be too large, though many variations are possible. Look in parks and on beaches for feathers. They are also available in craft stores, but often the prettiest are found ones. When deciding on the writing to go next to the feather, use appropriate wording, such as "with love" or "for you."

METHOD

1 Cut a piece of watercolor paper to suit the size of the feather and trim the edges with decorative-edge scissors. This piece should be smaller than the piece of mottled paper.

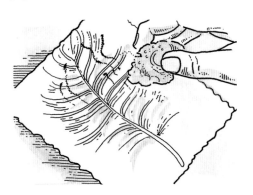

2 Spread glue along the spine of the feather, and press in place on the watercolor paper. Brush, dab, or stipple gold paint around the edges of the feather, on the paper, and then onto the spine of the feather.

3 Tear out a small scrap of photocopied writing. Stain this with diluted instant coffee to give it an antique effect, and glue it to the paper.

4 Tie the thread around the mounted feather like a present, knotting behind, and glue to the mottled paper. Glue to the front of the card.

MATERIALS

Feather Card
~
dark blue plain card, 6 × 8¼ inches, scored to fold in middle
•
watercolor paper
•
mottled light blue paper, cut to fit within front of folded card, and trimmed along edges with decorative-edge scissors
•
small piece of handwriting to complement card style, reduced on photocopier
•
feather
•
paintbrush or sponge
•
gold thread
•
gold or other color paint (powder and acrylic medium)
•
instant coffee
•
craft knife
•
cutting mat
•
decorative-edge scissors
•
fabric/paper glue

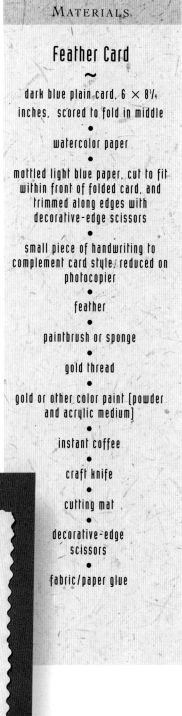

Introduction

You can make a print with almost anything — an apple sliced through the center makes a beautiful image, and what more evocative record of babyhood can you make than a tiny hand print in clay or on paper? Another simple method of printing unique images is mono-printing — simply roll oil-based printing ink on a sheet of glass, draw into the ink with fingers or the end of a paintbrush, gently press paper onto the ink, and lift up your print. A photocopier is one of my favorite "tools." Find a photocopy shop with a good machine which you can operate yourself.

You can feed through your own choice of paper — though it must always be cut square and be flat so that it does not block the machine. You can use

Printing and Painting

specially prepared acetate, and reduce or enlarge your images. This chapter also demonstrates some simple techniques such as potato cutting (which can look very professional when used with imagination), linoleum cutting (which is both exciting and inexpensive), and examples of other popular techniques such as embossing rubber stamps and using stencils.

Fall Scene
~

You can produce interesting and complex pictures to emboss by combining several different rubber stamps. These instructions can easily be adapted to design another card using a different combination of stamps.

METHOD

1 Score and fold the card into three sections, like an accordion – these will become the foreground, middle, and background. Open the card out.

2 Using brush markers, color directly onto the rubber surface of the picket fence stamp. Use bottle green for the fence shadow, pine green for the remainder. For the leaves, use brown, orange, and ocher, blending the colors on each leaf. When fully colored, breathe on the rubber surface of the stamp to re-moisten the ink, then stamp onto the white card all along the bottom edge of the left-hand section.

3 Color the fence using gray and dark gray markers. Cut out all of the white area above the fence in this section only.

4 Turn the whole card over so that the fence is face down. Stamp the neighborhood stamp centrally across the middle section. Ink the hilltop grass stamp with leaf green brush marker and stamp randomly below the houses. Now use the green marker and overstamp more grass. Use the stamp several times without re-inking to achieve shadings. Repeat using the ocher and bottle green markers.

5 Ink a sponge wedge with orange brush marker and sponge over the houses. Repeat with yellow. Using a fine black pen, draw frames at the house windows. Cut out above the houses in this section only.

6 Turn the card over so the fence is showing. On the right-hand section, stamp two tree frames using the brown and dark brown brush markers. Between them, stamp the sunshine stamp colored with cherry, orange, and yellow brush markers.

7 Ink the spring sprig stamp with leaf green and stamp randomly as for the grass, over the tree frame. Repeat with orange, ocher, and brown to fill the trees.

8 Ink the sponge with cherry and sponge around the sun. Re-ink with orange and sponge around the cherry ink, repeat with orange and yellow to create a sunset.

9 Fill the remaining area, under the trees, with more grass. Re-fold the card.

Sunflower Basket

~

Using one of the many embossing kits available from craft stores, and a heat source, such as a toaster, you can easily emboss on these rubber stamp images.

METHOD

1 Press the swirls stamp several times on to the inkstone embossing ink pad. Firmly press the stamp on the front edge of one of the folded cards. Lift straight up and only a slight, glistening image is visible.

2 Before the embossing ink dries, sprinkle with verdigris powder. Shake off the excess. Heat the embossing powder over a toaster or using a heat gun, until it melts and rises. Repeat for all four edges.

3 Stamp and emboss the wire basket on one side of the second card in the same way. Cut this out (including inside the handle) to leave a narrow white border.

4 Cut a rectangle 2½ × 4½ inches from one side of the second card. Draw the glue pen around the edge and sprinkle with embossing powder. Heat, then glue to the center front of the swirls card.

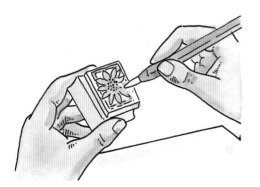

5 Using brush markers, color the surface of the sunflower stamp – the center brown, then edge one side of the petals only with ocher and blend with yellow. Breathe on the stamp to re-moisten, then stamp onto the back of the second piece of card. Repeat for another sunflower.

6 Cut between each petal to the center of the flower. Place the flower face down in your hand and, using a wooden spoon handle, rub the flower on the back to curl the petals. Turn over and bend each petal up slightly. Repeat for the other flower.

7 Apply small dots of brown liquid appliqué directly from the tube to the center section of each flower. Leave this to dry for a few hours. Heat, as if embossing, until the liquid appliqué puffs up.

8 Mount the wire basket and flowers on the swirls card using foam tape to give a 3-D effect. For a finishing touch, tie on a gold ribbon in a bow.

MATERIALS

Sunflower Basket
~

2 pieces 6 × 9 inches of white glossy card, one scored to fold in middle
•
Rubber Stampede stamps – sunflower mosaic, French wire basket, and swirls
•
inkstone and verdigris embossing powders
•
brown liquid appliqué
•
brush markers – brown, ocher, and yellow
•
4¾ inches gold ribbon
•
craft knife
•
cutting mat
•
foam mounting tape
•
wooden spoon
•
toaster or heat gun
•
glue pen

Ducks on the Pond
~

Potato prints are fun to make, whatever your age. This card uses a combination of potato prints, paper collage, and glitter. If small children make this card, they will need help and supervision with cutting.

METHOD

1 Cut the potatoes in half. Press potatoes onto paper towels to dry. With a soft felt-tip pen or the point of the knife, draw a star, a flower, a duck, and a small square on the potato surfaces. Cut away the potato around the shapes, leaving a raised pattern.

2 Lay the folded card on the blue paper and draw around the edge. Then, using a ruler and pencil, draw a frame ⅜ inch in from the edge of the paper. Carefully cut the frame out with the craft knife. Save the blue paper from the middle of the frame.

3 Cut wavy shapes from the lighter blue paper for the waves and sky. Cut a strip of grass and flower stems and leaves from the green paper. Glue to the card.

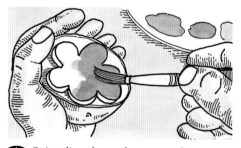

4 Paint directly on the potato shapes or spread out the paint with the roller on glass or perspex, and dip the potato shapes into it. Press firmly onto the card to make a pattern. When the prints are dry, use the square to print the middles of the flowers and the eyes of the ducks. Leave to dry.

5 Glue the blue paper frame to the edge of the card. Decorate the card with glitter glue, or spread or brush glue on the parts you would like to be glittery, and sprinkle the glitter on so that it adheres.

Fish and Starfish
~

Potato printing is one of the simplest of all printing techniques, usually taught to young children. However, with a little extra care in planning the design and choosing colors, the results can be surprisingly effective.

METHOD

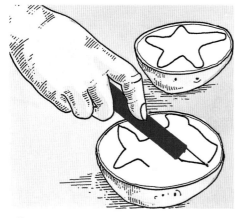

1 Cut the potato in half. Press potato halves onto paper towels to dry. Draw a fish on one half and a starfish on the other using a soft felt-tip pen or the point of the knife. Carefully cut away the parts of the design which you do not wish to print.

3 Trim the print to the size you want, and glue it to the blue card.

4 Print starfish around the border, using alternating colors.

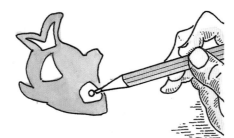

5 With the silver pen, draw a line around the edge of the fish print, and add silver dots for the fishes' eyes to make them shine.

2 Spread the paint with the roller on a smooth surface such as glass or plastic, and dip the fish shape into it so that it is covered with paint. Then press the fish onto the light-colored paper to make a print. Print other fish all over in a random pattern as if they are swimming, using different colors and cleaning the potato between each application of color. You can blend two colors of paint next to each other on the glass for multicolor fish.

MATERIALS

Fish and Starfish
~

blue plain card, 8½ × 12¼ inches, scored to fold in middle

•

smaller yellow paper for the fish print

•

poster, gouache, or acrylic paints in different colors

•

soft felt-tip pen

•

silver felt-tip pen

•

glass or plastic surface on which to spread paint

•

ink roller

•

potato

•

paper towels

•

craft knife or vegetable knife

Variation
Print a few fish or starfish on the envelope in which you are sending the card.

Print Repeat
~

For this design, the artist has used a small linoleum cut and printed it over and over again to build up a repeat pattern. You could also add a detail with another cut, printed in a contrasting color.

MATERIALS

Print Repeat
~

white plain card, 6¾ × 12 inches, scored to fold in middle

•

colored cardboard or paper cut slightly smaller than front of folded card

•

square of white paper for printing, cut just larger than linoleum

•

pencils

•

tracing paper

•

small square block of linoleum (or soft wood)

•

printing ink

•

sheet of glass or clear plastic for inking

•

ink roller

•

cutting tool

•

craft knife

•

cutting mat

•

masking tape

•

glitter glue (optional)

•

fabric/paper glue

METHOD

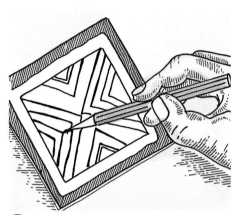

1 Draw the design for the linoleum cut on tracing paper. Scribble over the back of the drawing with pencil. Turn the drawing the right way up, place it on the block, and draw over the lines of the design again with a sharp pencil. This will transfer your design accurately to the linoleum.

2 Tape the edges of the linoleum to the work surface with masking tape. Cut around your design with a cutting tool. Don't forget that it is the parts which you *don't* cut that will be printed. Hold the cutting tool with two hands and rest your arms on the work surface, so that you have more control of the tool. Always cut away from you and *be very careful*, as the cutting tool will be very sharp. (It's a good idea to practice on a spare block first.)

3 Squeeze some ink on the piece of glass or similar surface. Roll the roller in the ink so that it is evenly covered. Then roll the ink evenly over the linoleum block.

4 Hold the block of linoleum carefully by the edges and press it down onto the square of white paper as if you were using a stamp. Repeat this process, inking the block each time, and carefully lining up the prints. Here, the cut has been given a quarter-turn each time, so that the pattern alternates.

5 When the finished print is dry, mount it onto the colored paper and decorate this with dots of glitter glue, if desired. Glue the paper to the card.

Christmas Print
~

For this design a single linoleum cut has been made for the whole picture. The card is printed in a slightly different way from the Print Repeat, which used a stamping method, and has been hand-tinted using colored inks.

METHOD

1 Follow Steps 1–3 from the previous card. You can trace a collage of images from books and magazines, or draw your own.

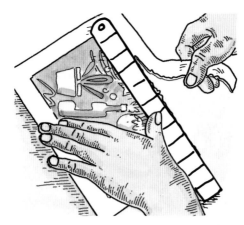

2 With the inked block still taped to the work surface, lay the tissue, or other paper, over the block, and very carefully press down, taking care not to move the paper. Tape the paper to the linoleum or work surface at the corners, and gently rub the back of the paper with the back of a spoon. This will make the images in the picture clearer.

3 Remove the paper from the linoleum, making sure you do not smudge the print, and allow it to dry.

4 Tint some areas of the print with the inks, allowing the colors to run into each other, and allowing some colors to be more intense than others.

5 Mount the tissue print on the white paper and then carefully tear the paper around the print, leaving a narrow border of white. The soft, irregular edge of the tissue gives the image a sense of movement, and the uneven border around the edge of the print adds a touch of interest.

6 Mount the finished design on the colored card using craft glue.

MATERIALS

Christmas Print
~

colored plain card, 8½ × 12 inches, scored to fold in middle
•
soft white paper to mount picture
•
white tissue paper, or a soft paper which gives an interesting ripped edge, for printing image
•
tracing paper
•
linoleum block cut to size of required image
•
metal spoon
•
printing ink
•
colored inks
•
sheet of glass or clear plastic for inking
•
ink roller
•
paintbrush
•
cutting tool
•
masking tape
•
craft glue

Silkscreen Card
~

This richly colored card is produced with stencils and a silkscreen. As the colors are printed separately, you must make a stencil for each color. It is important that these stencils are accurately traced from the master drawing so that the colors can be positioned correctly. When tracing, use a lightbox or a windowpane. Registration – positioning the different parts of the design so they don't overlap – can be difficult, so make sure your design is fairly open with spaces to see through.

MATERIALS

Silkscreen Card
~

precut card, 8½ × 12¼ inches
•
tracing paper
•
newsprint to make stencil
•
medium to lightweight silk,
8½ × 10½ inches
•
piece stiff cardboard, slightly
bigger than silk
•
printing dyes
•
silkscreen
•
silkscreen squeegie
•
spoon
•
craft knife
•
cutting mat
•
masking and gummed tape
•
iron-on adhesive

METHOD

1 Make a clear, accurate drawing and color-code it, using the template on p.125.

2 Trace a stencil for each color from newsprint and cut out, using the craft knife. Save the cutout pieces. They can be put back in place when you print other colors. Where necessary, leave small spaces between the cutting areas, which will help to keep the stencil whole. Make sure that the stencil is large enough to fill the screen, or the color will come through along the gap at the sides.

3 Clean and tape the edges of the screen to required size with gummed tape. Prepare dry silk for printing by stretching it on cardboard with masking tape – taut fabric gives the best results.

4 Mix printing dyes according to manufacturer's directions.

5 When ready, position stencil over the silk, ready to print with the first color. Any areas that you *don't* want to print should be masked by replacing the cutout pieces in the stencil. Lay the screen on top.

6 Using a spoon, pour the dye along the top edge of the screen and use the squeegie to pull it firmly down across the screen twice. You may need help to hold the screen down.

7 Remove the screen carefully. Wash the equipment to make it ready for the next color. When the colors are dry, repeat the process with subsequent stencils.

8 After printing is complete and the colors are dry, remove the fabric and iron on the back to set the colors. Score the card to fold in middle. Cut print along the edges and mount it with iron-on adhesive.

Variation
By using only one of the stencils and different colors, you achieve a very different effect.

Shell Print with Ribbon Tie

~

It's possible to make a great variety of cards using this method. Look in secondhand book stores for old prints – images from old cookbooks work well. Alternately, photocopy black-and-white drawings from books (make sure they're out of copyright). Cut the drawings out, mount them together, perhaps numbering or naming each item, and reduce on a photocopier to the size you want. Don't forget that you can also photocopy onto colored paper.

METHOD

❶ Brush the diluted coffee onto the print to "antique" it. Leave to dry.

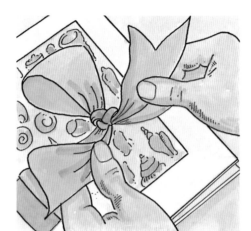

❸ Glue on the shell with all-purpose glue. Write your message, then tie a ribbon around the card to give it the feeling of a special gift.

❷ Use colored pencils to tint the print. Apply a thin layer of paper glue to the back of the print and quickly press it in place on the card mount. (It's useful to put pencil registration marks on the mount for the corners so that you can get it in the right position quickly.)

MATERIALS

Shell Print with Ribbon Tie

~

precut card, 8¼ × 6 inches, scored to fold in middle

•

photocopied print, reduced and cut to size

•

small shell

•

diluted instant coffee

•

colored pencils

•

paintbrush

•

ribbon

•

craft knife

•

cutting mat

•

fabric/paper glue

•

all-purpose glue

Striped Butterflies
~

Look for photographs or illustrations of bright or unusual butterflies in magazines or old books, and cut them out to decorate this card.

MATERIALS

Striped Butterflies
~

two pieces of thin cardboard,
6 × 8 inches
•
cutout butterfly motifs
•
acrylic paint in dark blue, red, and
green (or other contrasting colors)
•
gold felt-tip pen
•
paintbrush
•
small synthetic sponge
•
drawing compass
•
scissors
•
paper glue

METHOD

1 Paint one piece of cardboard dark blue, and the second piece red. Sponge them.

2 When dry, paint stripes in various shades of green over the red.

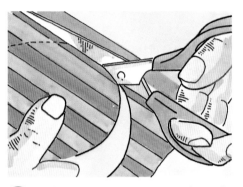

3 With the compass, draw a circle on the red and green card. Cut out and glue on to the dark blue card.

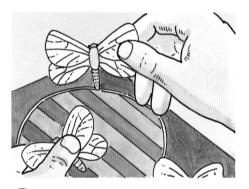

4 Arrange butterflies on the card, and glue in place.

5 Using gold felt-tip pen, draw carefully around the red and green circle.

Variation
Use different butterflies and background for another finish.

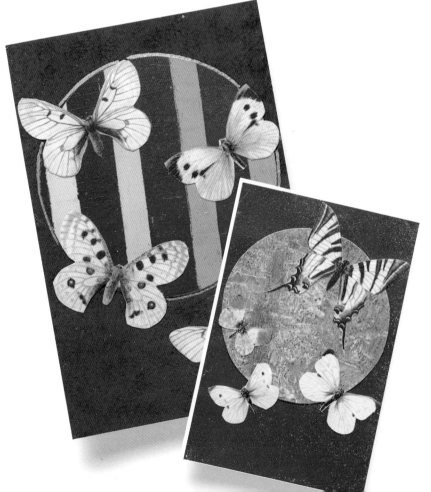

Leaf Print

~

Use a color photocopier to create an original and personal design. You can copy fresh leaves as well as dried: red and yellow autumn leaves look particularly striking.

METHOD

1 Arrange the leaves on the paper and attach them lightly with double-sided tape, or a spot of glue. Cover the picture with acetate and tape this to the backing paper at the edges with masking tape. The acetate protects the image and need not be removed when copying.

2 Have a color laser copy made, reducing the picture to fit. Cut it out and glue it to the front of the card.

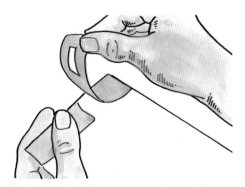

3 Tear a band along a cut edge of the contrasting paper. After signing the card, attach the paper band around it, using double-sided tape at the back so the band can slide off.

Get Fruity

You could experiment with the many 3-D painting craft products available, although this card was made with painter's modeling paste.

METHOD

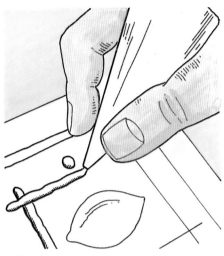

1 Put modeling paste in the piping bag, cut the corner off the bag and use the plain nozzle to pipe the 3-D pattern onto the card – you may wish to draw your picture with pencil first.

2 Allow the paste to dry for several hours, following the manufacturer's directions, then paint the fruit with a water-based paint.

MATERIALS

Leaf Print
~

plain card, 6 × 8¼ inches, scored to fold in middle

•

paper for mounting, same size as front of card

•

sheet of acetate

•

contrasting paper for band

•

selection of fresh or pressed leaves

•

double-sided and masking tapes

•

craft knife

•

cutting mat

•

paper glue

Get Fruity
~

plain card, 5¾ × 12¼ inches, scored to fold in middle

•

painters' acrylic modeling paste

•

strong piping bag for cake decorating, with plain nozzle

•

water-based paints – watercolor, acrylic, gouache, etc.

•

craft knife

•

cutting mat

Gallery

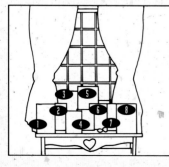

7 Double Sun
Underground Art
The designer of this card uses an original and unique process involving ceramic materials to create 3-D embossed images.

8 Native American Bird
Personal Stamp Exchange
This rubber stamp image of a bird is embossed and cut out, then hung by thread against an interesting mixture of paper backgrounds.

9 Vegetable Garden
Personal Stamp Exchange
Hand-colored and embossed vegetable stamps are printed on paper finished with decorative-edge scissors.

10 Easter Eggs
Kate Twelvetrees
This card uses cutout color photocopies, mounted on colored paper, covered with tissue paper and tied with raffia.

11 Peacock/Three Wise Men/Seahorses/Primitive Men
Julie Hammond
Hand-printed linoleum cuts are used in a variety of images, both simple and complex.

12 Flower and Print
Thérèse McDermott
This appliquéd fabric card has a handwritten and printed acetate background.

13 Chocolate Cake
Wendy Mackenzie
The cake on this card is printed using chocolate.

14 My Love is like a Red, Red Rose
Kate Twelvetrees
Antiqued photocopies and a dried rose make a lovely Valentine.

15 Dolphin Bay
Michael Bossom
Rubber-stamped dolphins border the central image, which is created with encaustic art – a technique that paints with hot colored wax.

16 Sparkler
Kate Twelvetrees
The black and white photocopy is from a nineteenth-century print. The card also uses a burnt-out sparkler, painted gold and wrapped with gold thread.

17 Heart and Words
Hand and Heart Design
Chinese gold and silver-covered tissue papers form frames for the heart and the print mounted on handmade paper backgrounds.

MATERIALS

Striped Flowers
~
two pieces of thin cardboard,
6 × 8 inches
•
cutout flower motifs
•
acrylic paint in cream and two
shades of blue (or two shades of
another color)
•
gold felt-tip pen
•
small paintbrush
•
craft knife
•
cutting mat
•
paper glue

Wrapped Color Print
~
plain card, 6 × 8¼ inches, scored
to fold in middle
•
color laser print
•
fine white tissue paper
•
contrasting paper for the band
•
craft knife
•
cutting mat
•
double-sided tape
•
paper glue

Striped Flowers
~

Magazines or gardening catalogs will provide a rich source of pictures for the central motifs of these cards.

METHOD

❶ Paint two pieces of cardboard in the two shades of blue.

❷ Paint cream stripes on the lighter blue card. Leave to dry.

❸ Arrange the flower motifs on the striped card, and glue in place.

❹ Carefully paint cream dots between lines with the small paintbrush.

❺ Fold the darker blue card in two, and using the craft knife and cutting mat, cut out a frame from this front half. Glue the decorated card in place behind it.

❻ Using the gold felt-tip pen, draw two lines framing the flower motifs. Draw gold dots in the middle of the cream dots.

Wrapped Color Print
~

Wrapping a color laser copy in tissue can make the drawing beneath look like an original. This pear is a detail from a nineteenth-century hand-colored engraving. Seal the card with a matching paper band after you have signed it, to complete your gift.

METHOD

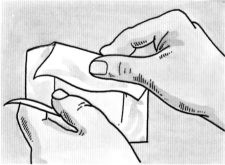

❶ Cut the color laser copy to size and wrap it in tissue, gluing the tissue to the back of the print. Glue the tissue package to the card.

❷ Tear a band from the edge of the contrasting paper, leaving one cut edge. After you have signed the card, secure the band around the card using double-sided tape at the back so that the band can slide off.

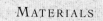

Two-tone Ferns

~

Use feathery fern shapes to make this simple card in two contrasting colors.

METHOD

Variation

1 Draw a pencil line down the middle of one piece of cardboard. Paint one half black and the other cream. Sponge with paint for interesting texture.

2 Arrange ferns in the center of the card. Use rolled-up masking tape to keep them in place or hold them firmly with your hand.

3 Sponge black paint over the fern on the cream side of the card, and cream paint over the fern on the black side. When dry, remove the ferns.

4 Fold the second piece of board and, use the craft knife and cutting mat to cut a frame from the front half. Paint one half black and the other cream. Place over the fern design, and glue in place.

Baby Clothes

~

Flocking powders are available from craft stores. The powder is usually sprinkled over a glued surface, but double-sided adhesive film has been used here.

METHOD

1 Cut a piece of film the same size as the front of the card. Peel off backing and stick to the card. Draw the outlines of baby clothes directly on the film.

2 Cut around the shapes you have drawn with a craft knife, taking care to cut only through the release paper. Peel off the background of the picture, leaving the objects covered. Sprinkle the card with the darkest flocking powder, gently rubbing it onto the film with your finger. Shake off excess.

3 Color-code the objects and peel the release paper off one color at a time, sprinkling each shape in the same way. Overlapping light colors onto the dark background gives a halo effect which softens the image.

Stenciled Hearts

~

You can buy stencils in many different shapes – but it's very easy to make your own.
A homemade stencil can be cut to any design you choose.

METHOD

1 Cut a heart-shaped window in the stencil board to make a stencil (see page 124).

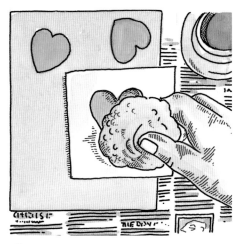

2 Place the stencil on the smaller of the pieces of colored paper. Press the sponge into the paint and test for density of color on a piece of scrap paper. Then, holding the stencil down firmly, press the sponge over the stencil. Allow to dry.

3 Place the stencil in a different position and spatter over it. To do this, dab the old toothbrush into fairly dry paint, and flick the brush over the stencil. Build up a pattern of hearts over the card, some sponged and some spattered.

4 Spatter a little pale-colored paint over the hearts and the background. Trim the composition if necessary.

5 Spatter the slightly larger piece of colored paper in a contrasting color.

6 Cover the piece of cardboard with foil, folding it over the edges, and gluing it in place at the back.

7 Using paper glue, attach the foil-covered shape, then the spattered paper, and finally the heart print, to the card.

Wax Crayon Heart

~

This simple but effective technique is fun for all ages and is a good method if you want fine detail. The heart-shaped window of this card frames the image in an unusual way.

METHOD

1 Cover the whole surface of the paper with different colored wax crayons in any random pattern you like.

2 Now cover the colored surface with black wax crayon.

3 Using the tip of the used ballpoint pen, draw a heart shape into the black wax crayon and scrape out a pattern revealing the colors beneath.

4 Trace the shape of the patterned heart, and transfer this outline to the front of the card. Cut out the heart-shaped window with scissors. Erase any pencil marks.

5 Spread glue along the inside edges of the window and press down in place around the colored heart. Make sure that the edge of the window is properly glued down all the way along. Glue the piece of blue lining cardboard to the back of the colored heart to cover it.

6 Decorate the front of the card with a simple pattern in black ink, if you wish.

Variation
Try making similar cards using different images, such as a simple star or flower. If you made the images smaller, you could even use two or more on the same card, either repeating a single design or combining different ones.

MATERIALS

Wax Crayon Heart

~

blue plain card, 5 × 8¼ inches, scored to fold in middle

•

thin white cardboard or paper, same size as front of folded card

•

blue cardboard to line inside front of card

•

tracing paper

•

wax crayons in bright colors, plus black

•

used ballpoint pen

•

eraser

•

scissors

•

craft knife

•

cutting mat

•

fabric/paper glue

MATERIALS

3-D Pearly Heart
~

orange card, 5½ × 11 inches, scored to fold in middle

•

1¾-inch square of white cardboard

•

3-D pearl fabric paint in different colors

•

scissors or craft knife

•

fabric/paper glue

Stenciled Sun Face
~

cream-colored plain card, 7 × 7 inches

•

thick stencil board, 8 × 8 inches

•

tracing paper

•

old newspaper

•

gold and bronze spray paints

•

craft knife

•

cutting mat

•

metal ruler

•

magic tape

3-D Pearly Heart
~

Using 3-D pearlized fabric paint, you can squeeze out a glossy, raised pattern with a pleasing irregularity of line on a card.

METHOD

1 Squeeze out a pearlized fabric-paint heart shape in the center of the white cardboard. Working out from the heart, build up your own pattern using different colors, leaving a white border around your design. Leave to dry long enough for the card to be handled.

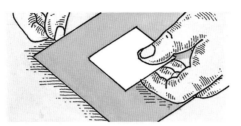

2 Glue the square to the orange card, placing it in the center.

3 Squeeze out a border in green along the white edges of the white square. Then, working outward, build up a wide, patterned border in other colors on the orange card. Allow the card to dry for 24 hours.

Stenciled Sun Face
~

This beautifully designed stencil makes a very impressive card. The spray paint gives a textured look of the quality of old gold. Accurate cutting of the sun's rays is essential, so use a sharp knife – but be careful.

METHOD

1 Trace the sun from the template (see p125) onto stencil board. Using the ruler, craft knife, and a cutting mat, cut away all the areas that are shaded on the template.

2 Cover the surrounding area with newspaper. Place the stencil over the card and tape in place with magic tape. Spray lightly with gold paint, then with bronze to fall mainly on the right-hand side of the stencil.

3 When the paint has dried, remove the stencil and cut out the rays of the sun with a craft knife.

Safety Warning
Always use spray paints according to the manufacturer's directions in a well-ventilated room and avoid inhaling them.

Flying Hearts
~

Printing with rubber stamps is another method of relief printing, like potato cuts. There are thousands of wonderful rubber stamps available, but you can make your own stamp by following this easy method. Simple shapes printed again and again to create a repeat pattern can look very effective. It works well on a small scale – the front of this card measures 3½ × 4½ inches.

METHOD

1 In felt-tip pen, draw a simple shape, such as a small heart with wings, on the eraser. To prevent the eraser from moving while you cut it, attach it to the mat using masking tape on all four sides. *Do not* hold the eraser while cutting. Using the craft knife, cut away the eraser around the shape to a depth of about ⅛ inch.

2 Cut two pieces of tissue paper to fit the front and back of the card. The front should be a different color from the back. Carefully glue the tissue in place, smoothing out any wrinkles.

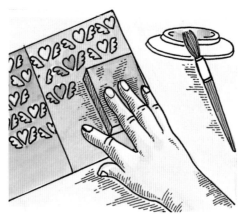

3 Use purchased ink pads, already impregnated with gold and silver ink; or apply water-based gold and silver ink to a flat kitchen sponge. Press the rubber stamp into the gold pad or paint gold onto the stamp, test on a piece of paper, then stamp a pattern all over the front and back of the card.

4 Clean the rubber stamp and cover the stamp with silver paint, then overprint silver on the shape in the center front of the card.

back

front

Variation
You could stamp a single print inside the card, and one on the flap of the envelope, to look like a seal.

Batik Print
~

This is an unusual way of using a well-known technique. Dye a larger piece of cloth and then cut out your favorite sections of the design to frame as cards, using cardboard in a coordinating color.

MATERIALS

Batik Print
~

pink plain card, 8¼ × 13½ inches, scored to fold in middle

•

white cardboard same size as front of folded card

•

piece of white cotton fabric 23½ × 23½ inches

•

old newspaper

•

batik wax

•

pink and blue cold-water dyes

•

bowls for dye

•

old saucepan

•

tjanting (available from craft stores)

•

craft knife

•

cutting mat

•

masking tape

•

fabric/paper glue

METHOD

1 Secure cloth on a flat surface with masking tape. Cover the surface with newspaper to protect it from hot wax.

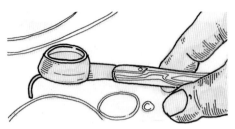

2 Heat the wax in a saucepan according to the manufacturer's directions. Draw on the cloth with the melted wax using a tjanting – the waxed areas will remain white. Allow to dry.

3 Mix the pink dye in a bowl and leave the cloth to soak as instructed in directions. Remove and rinse in cold water. Allow to dry.

4 Tape dry fabric as in Step 1. Apply wax to the areas to remain pink either with the tjanting or by dripping. Allow to dry.

5 Place cloth in a bowl with blue dye and leave as before. Rinse and leave to dry.

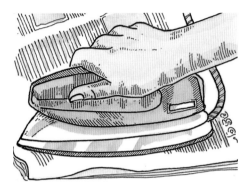

6 To remove the wax, first pick off as much as possible, then place newspaper under and over dyed cloth and iron carefully. The heat should melt the remaining wax, which will then be absorbed by the paper.

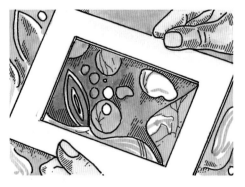

7 Cut out the desired piece of design and cut a window in the white cardboard to fit. Cut a second window in the front of the card, making the window slightly larger so that a border of white is left around the print. Glue the cards and the print together.

Classic Vase
~

The colors and bold patterns of this design are reminiscent of the ancient world. Look in your library for books showing old ornamental details – Egyptian, Greek, or Celtic designs perhaps – which could be simplified to make stencils, blocks, etc.

METHOD

1 Trace design from the template on page 122 onto the stencil board. Ordinary cardboard can be used, but oiled stencil board can be used again and again.

2 Cut out the shapes carefully with the craft knife on the cutting mat.

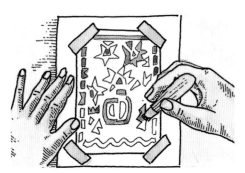

3 Attach the stencil with masking tape to the muslin. With the fabric pen, or brush and paint, fill in the black areas. Hold the stencil down to stop paint from seeping underneath.

4 Allow to dry and fill in the gold areas in the same way.

5 Cut a window from the black card to fit around your stenciled design. Apply glue to the back of the card and press it down in place on the muslin.

6 Paint some spare muslin gold and cut into strips for the border. Trim one long edge of each strip with the pinking shears.

7 Glue the gold muslin strips to the black frame. Glue the print and frame to the front of the black card.

MATERIALS

Classic Vase
~

black plain cardboard, 7½ × 12½ inches, scored to fold in middle
•
black card for window, same size as front of folded card
•
stencil board
•
tracing paper
•
muslin, slightly smaller than front of folded card, and spare strips
•
gold and black fabric pens, or gold and black paint and paintbrushes
•
pinking shears or scissors with a decorative edge
•
craft knife
•
cutting mat
•
masking tape
•
fabric/paper glue

Introduction

All you need is a sharp pair of scissors and a craft knife! There are many kinds of papercraft, and the techniques described here range from very simple torn shapes to cunning 3-D cards. If you enjoy making the pop-up and moving cards in this section, explore ephemera markets for different versions of pop-up cards that you can examine and copy. Remember childhood activities — rows of cut-out paper dolls, cutting "doilies," making paper chains at Christmas — adapt all the ideas you can. You can also experiment with tearing paper — textured or handmade papers reveal soft, feathery edges against darker backgrounds. Another increasingly popular technique is paper casting, demonstrated on

Papercraft

page 80. Visit specialist artists' and printers' paper suppliers, and look particularly at handmade papers containing natural materials such as flowers or straw. If paper cutting and collages really excite you, make your own paper using the simple methods described in paper-making books — each sheet you make will create more than one card and be truly individual. And you can experiment with the vivid colors of fabric dyes and printing inks.

Heart through the Window

~

You could use this technique to frame any interesting small image. For this particular card, tissue paper has been used for the heart so that it glows like stained glass when seen against the light. The blue also provides a vivid contrast to the orange.

MATERIALS

Heart through the Window
~

2 strips of colored paper in slightly different colors, each measuring approximately 6½ × 28 inches

•

small piece of blue paper approximately 1 × 1¼ inches

•

piece of blue tissue, slightly smaller than blue paper rectangle

•

iron-on adhesive or low-tack self-adhesive sheet

•

scissors

•

craft knife

•

cutting board

•

craft glue

METHOD

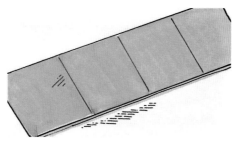

1 Using iron-on adhesive or a low-tack adhesive sheet and following the manufacturer's directions, attach the two long pieces of paper together.

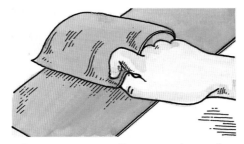

2 Score the strip lightly in three places so that you can accordion-fold the strip into four equal sides, each 7 inches wide.

3 Now cut irregularly shaped rectangular windows from the card by marking the corners and then draw in the sides of the first and largest window on the front of the card with a pencil. Cut out this shape, approximately 3¼ × 3½ inches wide, with scissors. Cut three more windows in the same way on each layer: they should become increasingly small so that the window in the back measures approximately ¾ × 1 inch.

4 Use the scraps of paper to make contrasting borders around the front and third windows.

5 Cut a tiny window in the shape of a heart from the blue paper and glue the blue tissue behind it. Apply a little glue to the edges of the smallest window on the back of the card and press it onto the blue paper.

Bon Voyage
~

Use this simple method to create pop-up cards for all kinds of events.

METHOD

1 Draw a plane and message banner lightly in pencil on the inside of the folded card, with the fold line running vertically through the center of both.

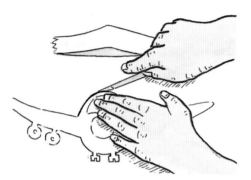

2 With the craft knife, carefully cut around the body of the plane, taking care not to cut through the sides of the body that meet the wings. In the same way, cut along the top and bottom edges of the banner, leaving the two ends uncut.

3 Erase any pencil marks and paint the plane and the banner. Allow to dry.

4 Gently pull the cutout shapes forward so that they fold in the opposite direction from the center fold. Fold the card.

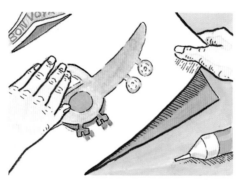

5 Spread glue on the back of the white card, leaving the cut-out sections unglued. Press in place on the blue card.

MATERIALS

Bon Voyage
~
plain white card, 6¾ × 8¼ inches, folded in half

•

same size rectangle of blue cardboard

•

watercolor paints

•

paintbrush

•

eraser

•

craft knife

•

cutting mat

•

fabric/paper glue

Stand-up Goose
~

Explore your local library for traditional folk-art illustrations and woodcuts which you could adapt to make other stand-up cards.

METHOD

1 Trace the outline from the template (see p122) onto the cardboard, allowing room to cut out the triangle in Step 4. Paint the areas that you want to remain white with masking fluid, and allow to dry.

2 Use a small sponge to apply the paint, carefully filling in each area, and allowing each color to dry before applying the next. Don't worry too much about going outside the main outline, as this will be trimmed. Paint in the eye with a fine brush. When the paint is dry, rub off the masking fluid.

3 Cut out the goose shape with a craft knife on a cutting mat.

4 Cut a 4-inch right-angle stand for the card, angling the short edge as shown. Score ½ inch in from the long edge. Fold back along the score line, and glue to the back of the goose.

5 For a shiny finish, or simply to protect the surface, varnish the painted goose using a diffuser and acrylic gloss or flat varnish.

Variation
You can also make a stand-up card from a photograph of a favorite object or toy. Photograph it against a white or plain background, enlarge the photo, and carefully cut out around the object.

Stand-up Pig
~

You could make your own template by tracing pictures or photographs of other animals from books or magazines. If you want a larger template, enlarge the image on a photocopier.

METHOD

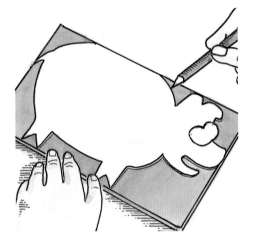

1 Fold the pink cardboard in half lengthwise, and lay the template (see page 123) on the board so that the back of the pig is on the fold. Draw around the template, and cut out the pig shape.

2 Glue on two circles of white cardboard for the eyes.

3 Draw on details either in pencils or with felt-tip pens.

3-D Star
~

This card has been made of thin cardboard with tissue paper glued to both sides to create an interesting mottled effect. Another way to achieve a similar result is to buy textured or patterned board.

METHOD

1 Following the manufacturer's directions, use the double-sided film or iron-on adhesive to cover both sides of the boards with dark blue tissue.

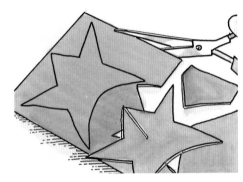

2 Using the template (see page 123), cut out two stars from the tissue-covered board. Make a slit in one star from the bottom to the center and in the other from the top to the center, as shown on the template. Slot the two stars together.

3 Place the star flat on the work surface. Use the iron-on adhesive to cover just the side facing you (it doesn't matter which side) with the light-colored tissue. The tissue will cover the slits where the two stars join, preventing the two stars from slipping apart, and providing a lighter-colored side on which to write a message.

4 Stick the small silver stars on the sides covered in dark blue tissue paper.

MATERIALS

Stand-up Pig
~

pink cardboard, 7 × 10 inches
•
tracing paper
•
scrap of white cardboard
•
colored pencils or felt-tip pens
•
craft knife
•
cutting mat
•
paper glue

3-D Star
~

two squares of thin cardboard, 8 × 8 inches
•
dark blue tissue paper to cover
•
light blue tissue for inside of card
•
small gummed silver stars
•
double-sided self-adhesive film or iron-on adhesive
•
scissors

Pop-up Sun, Bee, and Flowers

~

This cheerful card makes an intriguing summer birthday gift.

METHOD

back

1 Put the edge of one blue card abutting the edge of a green card and tape them together. Repeat with another two cards, then fold them together with the tape on the inside. Keep the cards open. Cut out each of the green cards, one in the shape of grass with a shrub on the right, one with a tree on the left. Make sure the fold is on the base and the grass is about 2½ inches high, with Card Two having grass over only two-thirds of the front (see above).

2 On the back of a blue card, make two horizontal parallel cuts, from the middle of the card to the grass side – one ⅜ inch, the other ¾ inch from the base.

3 On the back of Card Two, make two vertical parallel ⅝-inch cuts, starting ³⁄₁₆ inch from the bottom, the first 1⅛ inches and the second 1½ inches from the outside edge. Slot the grass side of the first card inside that of the second.

4 Open the cards out and thread the long, thin strip of Card One through the first slit of Card Two and back in through the second slit. Tape the loose end of the cutout strip closed, covering about ⅜ inch of the card. Pull the cards apart as far as they will go.

5 Make three little flowers by cutting out a clover shape from white paper with a small circle of yellow for the centers. Draw and cut out a sun and a bee. With the card still folded out face down and flat, place the flowers and bee face down between the two shrubs.

6 Glue a piece of blue button thread with strong all-purpose glue from the middle of one shrub to the flowers and the bee, and then to the second shrub. Make sure the thread is as tight as possible, then leave it to dry. Repeat with the sun, but in a higher position.

7 When dry, put more glue on the tip of each shrub and fold the back and front together. Let the card dry, then push the two halves together – the flowers, bee, and sun will fall down behind the grass unseen.

MATERIALS

Pop-up Sun, Bee, and Flowers

~

2 pieces green posterboard,
6 × 6 inches

•

2 pieces blue posterboard,
6 × 6 inches

•

yellow and white paper

•

blue button thread

•

craft knife

•

cutting mat

•

tape

•

fabric/paper glue

•

all-purpose glue

HAPPY
BIRTHDAY
× × ×

Sun through Clouds

~

Pull apart these two gray clouds . . . and the sun will come shining through.

METHOD

❶ Fold the two pieces of board in half lengthwise. Draw and paint cloud shapes on the front of each piece, with the fold forming the base of each cloud. Cut out.

❷ On the back of one of the cloud cards, make two horizontal parallel cuts from the middle of the card to the inner edge of the cloud, where it will touch the sun. One cut should be ½ inch from the fold at the base, the other cut should be 1 inch from the fold.

❸ On the back of the second cloud card, make two vertical parallel cuts ¾ inch long, starting ¼ inch from the fold. The first cut should be about 1¼ inch in from the sun side of the cloud, the second about 1½ inch in.

❹ With the inner sun sides together, slide the card with the horizontal cuts into the card with the vertical cuts. Open the cards out and thread the horizontal strip of the inner out and back in through the two vertical slits on the outer card.

❺ Tape the loose end of the horizontal strip back to the main body of the inner card. This will prevent the inner card from sliding right out of the outer card.

❻ Pull the cards apart as far as they will go, and measure the space between them about ¾–1¼ inches from the top of the clouds. Draw a sun, with rays, on the yellow card slightly larger than this measurement. Paint or draw in the features, and cut out.

❼ With the cards still opened out, and face down at full extension, place the sun, face down, between the front of the two cards, in the place it would be when risen.

❽ Join the sun to the clouds: glue a length of thread from 1¼ inches below the top of one cloud to the middle of the sun, to 1¼ inches below the top of the second cloud. Make sure the thread is as straight as possible, with no slack. Leave to dry.

❾ Dab glue near the top of each cloud inside the back and front, fold the cloud shapes back again, and press the tops together to close. Leave to dry, then slide the two clouds together.

MATERIALS

Sun through Clouds

~

2 pieces white posterboard,
10 × 12 inches

•

yellow posterboard

•

watercolor, gouache, or acrylic
paints for clouds and sun, or
colored pencils

•

paintbrush (if using paints)

•

strong thread

•

scissors

•

craft knife

•

cutting mat

•

masking tape

•

fabric/paper glue

New Baby Jacket
~

Stand this baby jacket up and you can rock it gently from side to side. The idea would also work well with cutout shapes of animals. If you don't have a punch which can make holes of varying sizes, use a paper hole punch for the ribbon holes and cut small diamond shapes in the card with a craft knife for a decorative effect.

MATERIALS

New Baby Jacket
~
blue cardboard, 7 × 12 inches
•
yellow paper, 6 × 7 inches
•
white cardboard, 6 × 7 inches
•
1 yard pink satin ribbon, ¼-inch wide
•
2 matching ready-made pink bows
•
4 animal-shaped buttons
•
needle and thread
•
pencil
•
hole punch
•
scissors
•
craft knife
•
cutting mat
•
tape
•
paper glue

METHOD

1 Make a template white cardboard for the jacket. Fold the blue cardboard in half lengthwise, and lay on the template so that the fold is on the neckline of the jacket. Cut another slightly smaller jacket shape from the yellow paper.

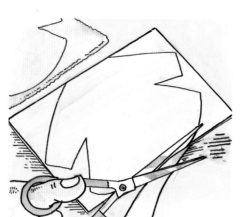

2 On the front of the jacket, mark a hole pattern with the pencil, and then punch out the holes.

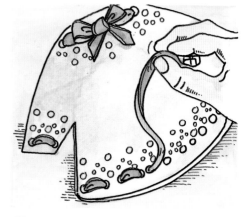

3 Thread pink satin ribbon through the large holes at the base, neck, and sleeves of the jacket (wrapping a small piece of tape around the end of the ribbon makes this easier). Secure the ends of the ribbon at the back with a little glue. Glue the two pink satin bows at the neck and bottom of the jacket.

4 Mark where the four buttons are to be placed on the front of the jacket, and punch holes at these points. Push the button backs through the holes and, with a needle and thread, join the buttons together on the back of the jacket. Secure the buttons and thread with tape.

5 Carefully glue the yellow paper shape to the inside front of the jacket to "line" it.

World of Clay

~

Although the world is modeled from clay, much of the interest of this card is in the paper cutting.

METHOD

1 Mold the shape of the world out of the modeling clay, then model the outlines of the continents and the lines of longitude and latitude. Leave to harden.

2 Fold the blue card into three equal sections. On the top section, draw a diagonal line from the top right-hand corner to the bottom left-hand corner of the top layer. Cut along the line.

3 Repeat with the other end section so that the two sections meet on a diagonal.

4 Place the world in the center of the card and trace around it on the two flaps. Remove the world and cut out the shape along the traced line.

5 Paint the hardened clay world and, when dry, give it a coat of clear varnish. Glue in position in the center of the card.

Fluffy-tailed Cat

~

Many different variations of this card are possible. The cat's tail will hang over the edge of the shelf on which the card is standing – the longer the tail, the better.

METHOD

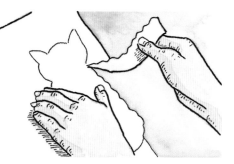

1 Lightly draw the rear outline of a cat on the watercolor paper. Tear carefully around this line – the soft paper gives the impression of fur. Erase pencil marks.

2 Glue the cat to the front of the card so that its bottom touches the bottom edge of the card. Apply a thin line of all-purpose glue around the neck of the cat and press the stones onto this.

3 Glue the end of the maribou trimming near the bottom of the card for the tail.

MATERIALS

World of Clay

~

blue card, 8¼ × 12 inches

•

self-hardening modeling clay

•

acrylic or water-based poster paint

•

modeling tool – a toothpick, flat-ended knife, or teaspoon handle

•

clear varnish

•

all-purpose glue

Fluffy-tailed Cat

~

plain card, 6 × 8¼ inches, scored to fold in middle

•

soft watercolor paper

•

small fake gemstones

•

12 inches maribou trimming

•

pencil and eraser

•

fabric/paper glue

•

all-purpose glue

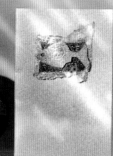
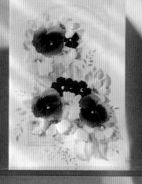

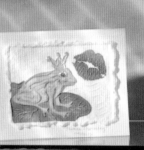

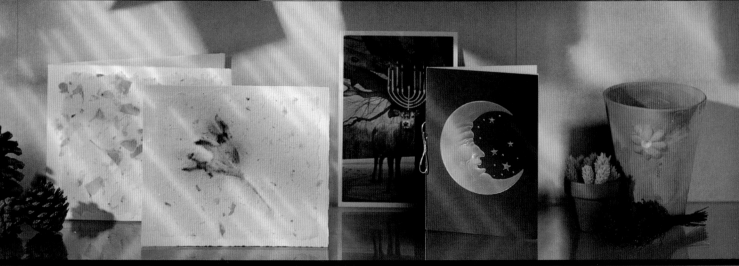

Gallery

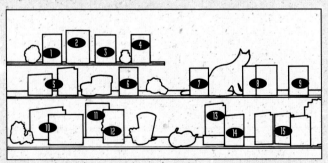

1 Fossil Fish
Helen Rowan
This handmade paper collage uses glitter paint to give the impression of fossilized stone.

2 Pansies
Wendy Beardmore
Cutout pansies, delicately spray painted for a realistic effect, are mounted on a printed background, in a picture adapted from Art Nouveau designs.

3 Porthole Fish
Jan Cooper
This 3-D card uses mirror board to create a porthole and suspends the fish on cotton thread against a sea background.

4 Mirror Mirror
Jan Cooper
Using mirror board again, this time with a frame card supported on cork pads, and wire arms and legs for a humorous effect.

5 Prince Charming/Angel
Roger Riege
Cast paper is used for low-relief sculpture molded, cast, and painted, then mounted on these two cards.

6 Papercast Shells
Rachel Purser
A more complex version of the starfish card (see page 80), using the same papercasting technique.

7 Ladybug

Rosalind Miller

The ladybug is printed in black and then loosely overprinted in red, with echoes of Japanese woodcuts.

8 Handmade Paper Reliefs

Penny Saxby

These two cards use treated handmade paper, washed and tinted with color, as a background for collages of pressed flowers, fabric scraps, and metal.

9 Happy Birthday

Susan Coomer

Magazine scraps, some tied with thread as "presents" and one minute envelope complete with stamp, are used on a tiny scale in this unusual card.

10 Petal Paper

Olive Dean

Recycled computer paper and flowers from the designer's backyard are the ingredients of this lovely paper, which is mounted on a deckle-edged background.

11 Happy Hanukkah!

Joan Hall

A humorous photomontage using magazine scraps to celebrate Hanukkah.

12 Man in the Moon

Paper Troupe

Embossed moon and stars are collaged onto a midnight background.

13 Church Wedding

Julie Dean

A paper collage using torn photocopied images, with one section mounted on cardboard for a slightly 3-D effect.

14 Paper Flower

Sophie Williams

Contrasting papers and threads are machine stitched onto a dyed paper background.

15 Teddy Bears

Mayhem Designs

These cut paper collages use a variety of brightly colored papers for children's cards.

Apple Card
~

The accordion folds of crêpe paper in this card are easier to make than they look. Choose a fresh apple green for the crêpe paper, and a darker green for the outer "skin."

MATERIALS

Apple Card
~
green cardboard and white
cardboard, each 5 × 7 inches
•
25 pieces of green crêpe or tissue
paper, same size as the cardboard
•
scraps of black paper
•
green colored pencil
•
needle and white thread
•
craft knife
•
cutting mat
•
craft glue

back

front

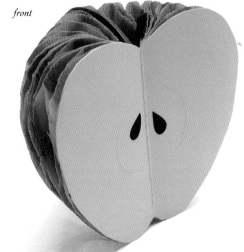

METHOD

1 Make a "sandwich" with the green card at the bottom, the white card on top, and the green papers in between. Draw a line down the center of the white card, and sew the layers together along this line, green side uppermost, using backstitch, and finish off leaving 1¼ inches of card and paper unstitched at each end.

2 Fold in half with the green card on the outside. Draw a half apple shape on one half of the green card. Cut it out through all the layers using the craft knife and mat.

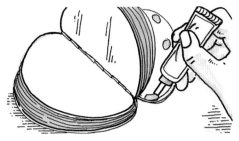

3 Open out one half of the card. Lift the bottom layer of crêpe paper off the white card and place three evenly spaced spots of glue around the edge of the white card.

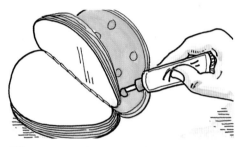

4 Press the first layer of paper onto them and allow to dry. Then glue the next layer of paper to the first in the same way, using only two spots of glue placed between the three spots on the first piece. Repeat with each layer of paper, using three and two spots of glue alternately, and gluing the last piece to the green card. Repeat the whole process on the other side.

5 Cut out two tear-drop shapes from black paper and glue them in the center of the white card as seeds. For the core, draw two green semicircles with a colored pencil. Glue a black cutout stem at the top of the apple under the crêpe paper.

Sea Monster
~

This ingenious but simple method of gluing paper circles together could be used in many different designs. This would be a good technique to teach children. Try this method for snowman Christmas cards.

METHOD

1 Cut out a wavy shape from the blue board using scissors or a craft knife.

2 For the top of the body, use scissors to cut 15 circles of each color tissue paper with a 1-inch diameter. For the center, cut 15 circles of each color with a ¾-inch diameter. For the tail, cut 15 circles of each color with a ½-inch diameter.

3 To assemble each part of the body, glue alternating colored circles of tissue together. Dab four spots of glue around the edges of the circle, but put these glue spots at alternating points on the next circle and continue in this way.

4 Fold the blue board in two places, near the center and the tail. Glue the tail over the fold, so that the tissue becomes flat when accordion-folded. Repeat for the center.

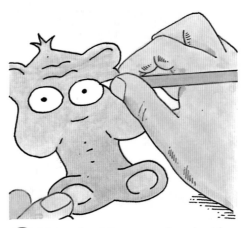

5 Make a head from green board, with white eyes and felt tip details. Glue one end of the top body to the blue card, and the other to the back of the monster's head.

MATERIALS

Sea Monster
~
blue posterboard, 5¼ × 11 inches
•
two contrasting colors of tissue paper
•
green and white posterboard 2¾ × 4 inches
•
felt-tip pens
•
scissors or craft knife
•
cutting mat
•
fabric/paper glue

Big Mouth Hippo

~

Open this card, and this hippo will stick out his tongue at you.

MATERIALS

Big Mouth Hippo

~

plain card, 5 × 12 inches

•

pink paper, same size as card, or pink paint

•

white paper

•

red paper

•

black, gray, and white paint

•

paintbrush

•

scissors

•

craft knife

•

cutting mat

•

ruler

•

fabric/paper glue

METHOD

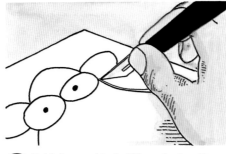

1 Fold the card in half lengthwise. Draw a hippo's head on the front. Give him a great big nose and a pair of jutting-out teeth. Using a craft knife, cut around the hippo's head through both layers of card.

2 Paint the front and back of the head gray, adding the details of eyes, nostrils, ears, and outlining in black.

3 Fold the pink paper. Using the hippo head as a template, draw around it on the pink paper. Cut out two pink paper shapes, and glue to the inside front and back of the head – or just paint the inside pink.

4 With the ruler and blunt edge of the scissors, score a line across the front of the face, about ¼ inch below the eyes. Fold the lower part of the face back up from this line. Draw a pencil line along the fold, on the other half of the card.

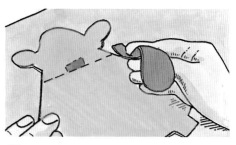

5 Cut out a tongue from the red paper. Glue it to the inside of the mouth, just above the pencil line on the back card.

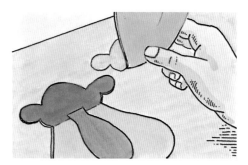

6 Spread glue on the inside of the head, as far down as the pencil line. Press the two top halves of the head together, enclosing the top of the tongue, but leaving the mouth open.

7 Paste white paper teeth inside the mouth (and on the back of the jutting teeth). Cut out a black paper epiglottis and glue in place, or paint a black epiglottis.

Loopy Lion
~

Turn the mane of this lion, and watch his expression change.

METHOD

1 Using the compass, draw two circles with a 5-inch diameter, one on the white card and one on a yellow card. Make sure there is at least a 1-inch border all around the outside of the yellow circle. Mark the center of each circle on the back.

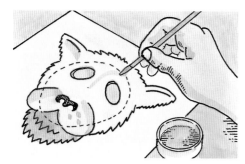

2 Cut out the white circle. Draw and paint a lion's face (without the mane) on the yellow circle, making sure that the outline of the face is just bigger than the marked circle. The eyes should be fairly large and close together, toward the top of the head. Cut out the face and make two windows for the eyes.

3 Now make the mane. Draw another circle on the other yellow card, 9 inches in diameter. Draw and paint the mane, and then cut out. Pierce a small hole in the center of the mane.

4 Glue the top of the binding pin to the center back of the lion's head. Leave to dry, and tape over it so it won't come loose.

5 Pierce a small hole in the center of the white circle. Glue the white circle to the mane, making sure that the holes in the center align.

6 With the white circle uppermost, push the ends of the pin on the back of the face down through the center of the white circle and the mane.

7 Working through the eye holes, draw different pairs of eyes, showing different expressions. Draw the first pair, then turn the mane until the eye spaces are blank again and draw the next pair, and so on until you return to the first pair. Check that all the expressions are correct and that none overlap, then take the face and move apart again. Paint in all the pairs of eyes.

8 Push the ends of the pin through the middle of the square of green cardboard. Secure the ends with glue and, when the glue is dry, tape over to make sure that the pin is firmly attached.

9 Glue the green square to the front of the card, with the opening on the right.

MATERIALS

Loopy Lion
~

plain green card,
10 × 20 inches, scored to fold in
middle of long side
•
10 × 10 inch square of matching
green cardboard
•
2 yellow and 1 white cards,
10 × 10 inches
•
watercolor, gouache, or acrylic
paint for lion's eyes, features,
and fur
•
paintbrush
•
drawing compass
•
binding pin with wide, flat head
•
scissors
•
craft knife
•
cutting mat
•
masking tape
•
paper glue

Starfish
~

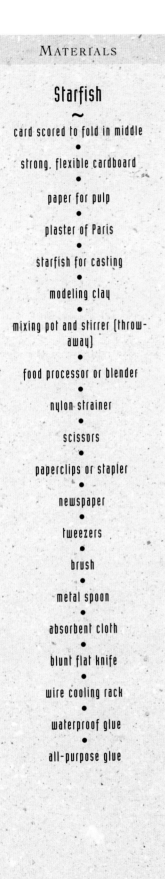

MATERIALS

Starfish
~

card scored to fold in middle
•
strong, flexible cardboard
•
paper for pulp
•
plaster of Paris
•
starfish for casting
•
modeling clay
•
mixing pot and stirrer (throw-away)
•
food processor or blender
•
nylon strainer
•
scissors
•
paperclips or stapler
•
newspaper
•
tweezers
•
brush
•
metal spoon
•
absorbent cloth
•
blunt flat knife
•
wire cooling rack
•
waterproof glue
•
all-purpose glue

It is easiest to use lightly or non-printed paper when first making recycled paper pulp. Photocopy or computer paper is ideal.

METHOD

1 Tear the paper into small pieces no bigger than ¾ inch square and soak in a bowl of water for several hours. When soft, macerate the paper in a food processor or blender. Take one cup of paper and two of water at a time and blend until the fibers separate and form a "pulp." Transfer the pulp into a nylon strainer. Allow to drain, but not dry out.

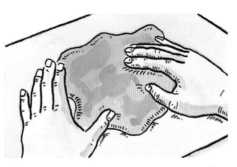

2 Warm and then press out a piece of clay so that it is slightly larger than the starfish. It should be about ⅜–¾ inch thick. Gently press the starfish halfway into the surface of the clay.

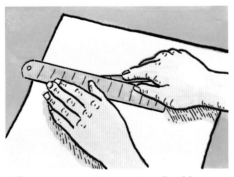

3 Cut a strip of strong but flexible cardboard at least 2 inches longer than the height of the clay with the object pressed into it and large enough to wrap tightly around the clay, making a collar. Secure with paperclips or staples. Place on newspaper on a flat surface.

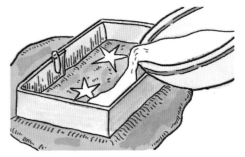

4 Mix the plaster powder to a thick, creamy consistency with water in a throw-away container, then pour carefully over the object. The tight cardboard collar will stop the plaster from escaping. (Any leaks can be checked by pressing a spare piece of clay against the cardboard.) Tap the cardboard collar to help release any air bubbles. Leave to dry and harden.

5 Remove the cardboard collar and carefully pull off the clay. The object should come away. If it doesn't, release it by carefully easing or levering it out with tweezers. When the plaster casting mold is totally dry and hard, brush a very thin layer of waterproof glue over the casting surface. Leave to dry.

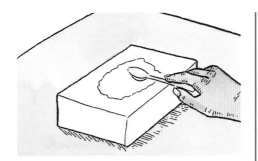

6 Spoon a small amount of the drained paper pulp onto the casting surface of the plaster mold. Using the back of a spoon, press the pulp into and over the mold. Use an absorbent cloth to press down firmly on the pulp, removing all excess water and pushing the pulp into the shapes on the casting surface.

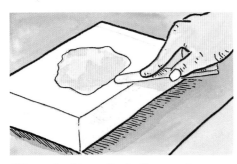

7 With a blunt, flat knife, ease the paper pulp cast off and out of the plaster mold. Leave in a warm place to dry, preferably on a wire cooling rack. Mount it on the card using a strong all-purpose glue.

Windows on the World
~

This card has been made using a purchased rubber stamp. Here, the stamp has a globe design, but you could use any motif. The card is lined with white paper. It is much easier to write a message on this white lining, and the tissue prints look much brighter against the white background.

METHOD

1 Cut three windows in the card front using the craft knife and cutting mat.

2 Cut pieces of tissue paper to fit inside these windows with a narrow border. Stamp with white ink onto the pink and purple tissue. Stamp onto scrap paper until all the ink is used up and, if necessary, clean the stamp with a little water. Stamp onto the orange paper with black ink.

3 Apply a little glue around the inside edges of the windows, and carefully press down onto the tissue prints.

4 Apply a thin line of glue inside the card next to the fold on the right-hand side and glue the folded white paper along this line.

MATERIALS

Windows on the World
~
plain black card, 8¼ × 12 inches, scored to fold in middle
•
white paper, cut to the same size as the card and folded in middle
•
pink, purple, and orange tissue paper
•
black-and-white ink pads which have water-based inks
•
rubber stamp
•
scissors
•
craft knife
•
cutting mat
•
fabric/paper glue

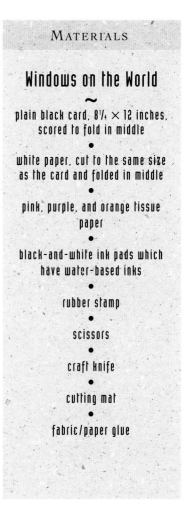

Pop-up Snowflake
~

The snowflake motif on the front of this card and the pop-up snowflake inside make a special card for Christmas.

MATERIALS

Pop-up Snowflake
~

plain white poster board,
6 × 12 inches, scored to fold in
middle of long side
•
2 sheets white typing paper,
8 × 10 inches
•
6½ × 12½-inch piece marbled blue
paper
•
newspaper
•
pearl blue spray paint
•
drawing compass
•
scissors or craft knife
•
cutting mat
•
double-sided tape
•
magic tape
•
fabric/paper glue

front

inside

METHOD

1 Using a compass, draw a circle with a radius of 2¾ inches on one of the pieces of white paper. Next, divide the circle into six segments, marking with your compass the radius around the circumference, and joining the marks with straight lines through the center.

2 Carefully cut out the circle with scissors or a craft knife. Fold the circle in half along one line, then along the other two lines so you end up with a folded triangle shape with a curved base.

3 With the craft knife and cutting mat, cut geometric shapes within the folded triangle, making sure that you leave the two outer straight edges uncut. Unfold your "snowflake."

4 Loosely attach the snowflake to the front of the card with magic tape. Place the card on newspaper to protect the work surface, and spray from a distance of about 12 inches from side to side if you want the paint even, or from the center out if you want a graduated effect as shown here. Leave to dry, then carefully remove the snowflake stencil.

5 Glue the marbled blue paper to the inside of the card, trimming the edges as necessary. Repeat Steps 1, 2, and 3 to make a different snowflake for the inside.

6 Once you have unfolded your snowflake, take one segment, and crease the opposite way in the center. Crease the opposite segment in the same way.

7 To attach the snowflake to the card, add two small tabs of paper measuring approximately ⅛ × ¼ inch with double-sided tape, or glue. Center the snowflake top and bottom inside the card. You will need to experiment to find the best position for the snowflake, depending on how flat you want it to open out. First attach one tab to the card; then close up the snowflake and then the card, and press – this way, you should be able to attach the snowflake evenly.

Daisy Card

~

This circular card with the flower motif looks unusual, but is extremely easy to make. When cutting out the petals, avoid giving them a uniform shape. Make some slightly wider and longer than others, and arrange them in an irregular way around the heart – as they would be in their natural state.

METHOD

1 Fold the blue board in half. Using the compass, draw a 6-inch circle on the folded board. Allow the circle to overlap the fold slightly on one side. Cut out the circles, making sure they are still joined along the flattened edge.

2 Cut a 2-inch circle from yellow card for the heart of the flower. Lightly draw a 1¼-inch circle in the middle of the blue board. Glue to the center front of the card.

3 Cut individual petals from the watercolor paper, 3–4 inches long and ½ inch wide in the middle. The top edge of each petal should be straight. Dab glue at the top of each petal and press in place around the 1¼-inch circle in the middle of the heart, allowing the petals to overlap each other, leaving the ends loose.

Flower Heart

~

The real flower seeds in the center of this card are placed loose in a clear plastic bag, and move as the card is moved. Put the name of the plant inside the card, with instructions for sowing.

METHOD

1 Attach double-sided film to the front half of the brown paper. Draw a circle in the center and draw petals radiating out from this. Cut out the petal shapes, leaving the center uncut.

2 Carefully peel back a narrow strip of the film at the top of the card and stick this strip to the white card, placing it accurately. Gradually peel back the film, sticking the cutout flower to the white card, bit by bit.

3 Cut out the center of the flower through both layers.

4 Put the seeds in the plastic bag and tape it to the inside of the card so that the seeds are visible through the hole.

MATERIALS

Daisy Card

~

blue posterboard, 7 × 14 inches

small piece yellow posterboard

watercolor paper

drawing compass

scissors

paper glue

Flower Heart

~

white card with a textured finish, 5½ × 11 inches, scored to fold in middle

brown paper, cut to the same size as the whole card

double-sided self-adhesive film

seeds

small clear plastic bag

craft knife

cutting mat

tape

Birthday Scroll
~
This card unrolls into a cheerful birthday banner.

METHOD

1 Cover the white card with orange tissue paper using iron-on adhesive. Mark the card halfway down the long side and measure and mark each of these halves into three equal sections to make six altogether. Fold the card along these lines to form a scroll with the orange paper on the inside.

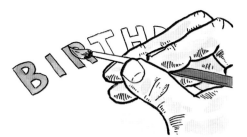

2 On the white side, on the third section from the bottom, write the word "happy." The base of the letters should touch the fold. Using a craft knife and cutting mat, cut around the top and sides of the letters, but do not cut the bottom edge of the letters, which should remain attached to the fold line. Turn the card over to the orange side and push the letters through and stand up.

3 Cut the word "birthday" from white card. Paint blue, allow to dry, and glue to the section of the orange card below the cutout "happy."

4 Put a piece of scrap paper under the stand-up "happy" and paint the letters blue. Allow to dry. Using iron-on adhesive, glue the blue tissue to cover the white side of the card. The "shadow" of the word "happy" is now a transparent tissue window. Roll up the scroll and tie with ribbon.

Bubbly Fish

~

Pull out the tabs on the right-hand side of this fish, and watch the bubbles coming from the fish's mouth.

METHOD

1 Draw a fish shape, without a bottom jaw, on the orange board. Draw a bottom jaw with a fin on the end. Both parts should be facing right.

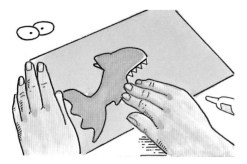

2 Cut out teeth from the white board, and glue to the top and bottom jaws. Glue the main body of the fish to the left-hand side of the blue board. Glue on a pair of eyes, marking the pupils with the felt pen.

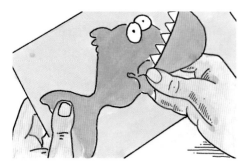

3 Using a strong glue, attach the binding pin to the back of the bottom jaw, behind the fin. Push the pin through the body of the fish and the board, so that the jaw swings from the fin. Fold the pin legs out behind the board.

4 Using the craft knife and ruler, cut three pairs of vertical slots on the blue board to the right of the fish.

5 Cut three strips of blue board to slide between the slots. They should be slightly narrower than each pair of slots, and long enough to reach from the right-hand edge of the card to the middle.

6 Cut out three circles of white paper, and glue these to the left-hand end of the strips. Cut three tabs of orange board, and glue these to the other end of the strips. Slide the strips into the slots.

7 Glue another piece of blue board as a backing to the main board. Do not attach it on the right-hand edge and take great care not to get any glue on to the slots or the strips, or you won't be able to slide the strips in and out.

MATERIALS

Bubbly Fish
~

3 sheets of blue posterboard,
8 × 12 inches
•
1 sheet of orange posterboard,
8 × 12 inches
•
sheet of white paper or thin
cardboard
•
binding pin with wide, flat head
•
pencil and felt-tip pen
•
scissors
•
craft knife
•
cutting mat
•
ruler
•
all-purpose glue
•
fabric/paper glue

Introduction

Throughout history, pictures have been made using fabric and stitchery. The ancient Egyptians used appliqué, and in past centuries in the West, girls as young as five stitched their first samplers. There are all kinds of techniques to explore, whether you are an experienced dressmaker or embroiderer or have never stitched in your life. In the latter case, follow the simple instructions or make the cards using glue.

Felt is easy and fun because it doesn't fray while, by fraying silk, you can create a beautiful background. Visit and enjoy the magic of fabric stores and notions counters with a new eye for detail — perception changes when you need such small quantities and you can buy the best. You can use fabrics

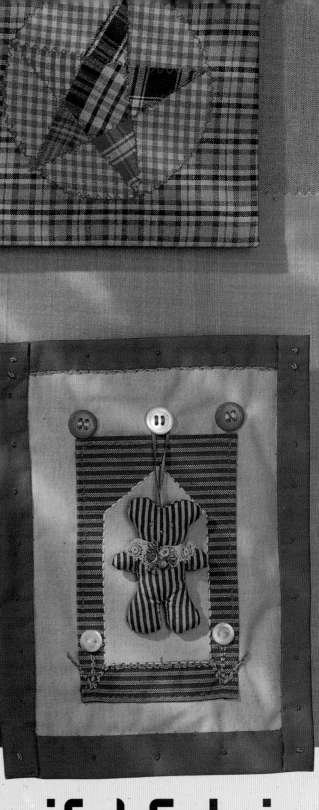

Fanciful Fabric

right across the selection, from hand-embroidered silk to vividly colored man-made fabric. Alternately, rummage in scrap bags for remnants, buttons, and ribbons. Explore craft museums and look through library books for examples of exquisite antique quilts, patchwork, and embroidery, and collect pictures of borders, color combinations, and motifs to act as an inspiration for your cards.

Felt Cornucopia

~

The vibrant colors and bold shapes are what first strike the eye on this card. The addition of embroidery stitches, however, is a vital part of this design, providing depth and detail.

MATERIALS

Felt Cornucopia

~

plain card. 7 × 11 inches, scored to fold in middle

•

tracing paper

•

white or pastel felt for background. 5¹/₂ × 7 inches

•

small pieces of felt in various colors

•

embroidery threads in several colors

•

embroidery needle

•

scissors

•

double-sided tape or fabric glue

METHOD

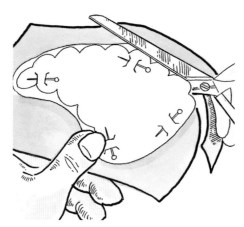

1 Draw the cornucopia on tracing paper and cut out the shapes. Use these in turn as a guide to cut out the cornucopia, leaves, stems, fruit, and flowers from the colored felt pieces.

2 Glue the cornucopia to the background felt, and assemble the other pieces, gluing each in turn. Pieces that lie behind other pieces, such as the stems behind the fruit, should be stuck down first.

3 Add detail to the leaves and outline the main shapes with simple embroidery stitches, using three strands of thread and contrasting colors.

4 Attach the finished picture to the front of the card either with double-sided tape, or with fabric glue applied thinly.

Variation
Try other shapes in your felt collage. An arrangement of shells would work well, for example.

Window with Lace Curtains
~

This card uses a mixture of solid and printed fabrics and simple embroidery to give an interesting effect.

METHOD

1 Iron flowered fabric onto iron-on adhesive. Cut around the flower shapes. Remove paper backing from adhesive, and iron floral fabric onto one of the solid ones.

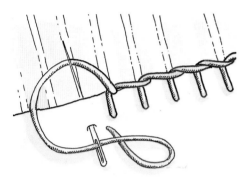

2 Fold over and iron a hem at the top of both pieces of solid fabric. Lay it behind the fabric with the flowers, and the striped fabric behind this. Pin these layers together. Sew blanket stitch over the two seams with the cream thread.

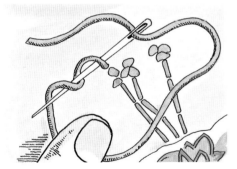

3 Using green embroidery thread and backstitch, sew on flower stems. With pink and blue thread, sew large French knots to look like flower buds, and sew petals in lazy daisy stitch. Sew two birds in the sky with gray thread and backstitch. Make sure that these embroidered features will all fit within the window.

4 Place a strip of lace on each side of the picture and baste lightly at top and bottom. Apply glue to the inside edges of the window, and press down in place over the picture.

5 Glue the backing to the window portion of the card. Glue on the two bows.

MATERIALS

Window with Lace Curtains
~

three-panel cream precut card with cut-out window, with 5 × 6¾-inch front

•

2 plain, 1 striped, and 1 flowered pieces of fabric

•

iron-on adhesive

•

1-inch-wide lace strips

•

2 purchased cream satin bows (or make your own)

•

green, pink, blue, gray, and cream embroidery thread

•

embroidery needle

•

scissors

•

fabric/paper glue

Quilted House
~

This is a house-moving card in a quilted frame. If you are sending it to someone you know well, perhaps you could add extra appliquéd details relating to their family or new home.

MATERIALS

Quilted House
~

plain card, 6¾ × 11½ inches, scored to fold in middle
•
rectangle of thin cardboard, fractionally smaller than front of card
•
plain peach-colored fabric
•
muslin
•
patterned fabric
•
thin batting
•
iron-on adhesive and iron
•
narrow peach-colored satin ribbon
•
2 purchased bows to match ribbon
•
thread to match patterned fabric
•
needle and thread, or sewing machine
•
scissors
•
pinking shears (optional)
•
craft knife
•
cutting mat
•
fabric/paper glue

METHOD

1 Cut a piece of muslin slightly smaller than the backing card, and glue it to the card at the edges.

2 Cut out a house from the patterned fabric, and a roof and windows from the peach. Glue to the center of the muslin using iron-on adhesive. Frame with four strips of ribbon, glued lightly in place.

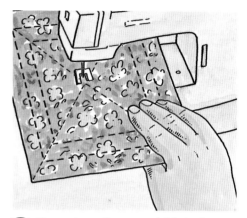

3 Cut a piece of patterned fabric about 1 inch bigger than the backing card. Sandwich a piece of batting between this and a similar-sized piece of muslin. Stitch across this in lines to make a quilt. Stitch diagonal lines from each corner. Cut a square from the center of the quilted fabric and turn a hem under so that the quilting frames the house and ribbons. Glue the quilted frame over the muslin, folding the quilting over onto the back of the backing card, and gluing the edges.

4 Cut other small shapes from the plain peach fabric and from the patterned fabric, and iron them onto the frame in the same way as before.

5 Glue the two small bows to the frame.

6 Glue the quilted picture to the front of the card.

Scented Heart

~

If you do not want the card to look bare when the scented heart is removed, add another motif beneath it.

METHOD

1 Cover the rectangle of thin board with the fabric, folding it behind the card and securing it with glue or tape.

2 Sew a border of lace around the edges of the card, pleating it at the corners. Sew on a cream bow at each corner.

3 Make a loop of ribbon and sew one end to the back of the padded heart and the other end to the back of the blue bow. Sew the blue bow to the fabric-covered card, so that the heart hangs just below the center of the card.

4 Glue the finished collage on the front of your card.

5 If using, sew or glue a lace heart or other motif to the fabric where it will be covered by the padded heart.

MATERIALS

Scented Heart
~

plain card, 8¼ × 12 inches, scored to fold in middle

•

thin cardboard, the same size as the front of the plain card

•

fabric to cover thin board

•

purchased heart sachet

•

purchased lace heart or other motif to go under padded heart (optional)

•

lace trimming

•

4 cream bows

•

blue bow

•

narrow satin ribbon to match blue bow

•

needle and thread

•

scissors

•

craft knife

•

cutting mat

•

masking tape or cellophane tape

•

fabric/paper glue

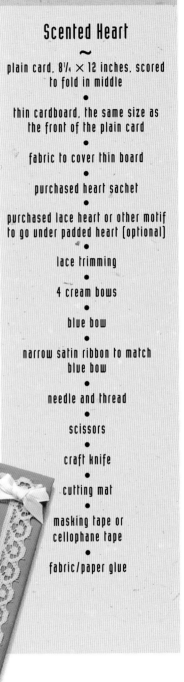

Teddy in the Window
~

The attractive feature of this card is that the teddy, preferably filled with potpourri, can be removed from the card. You could include a small, appliquéd motif under the teddy, so that if it is removed the card will still make a picture.

METHOD

1 Cut muslin to cover card for background. Pin on blue-striped fabric, turning edges under. Sew fabric in place using backstitch and blue thread.

2 Iron adhesive onto a small piece of muslin. Draw house shape. Cut out and iron this onto striped fabric.

3 Sew on the buttons and embroider green leaves around two lower buttons. Sew a border around the edge of the house with cream embroidery thread.

4 Place whole muslin house and backing in center of large piece of blue fabric. Fold edges of blue fabric in over the muslin, turning to form a hem, and sew in place with blue thread.

5 With embroidery thread, sew blue french knots at 1-inch intervals. Sew two green knots at the top corners, and one each at the bottom. Using green thread, sew two lines of backstitch at top of picture.

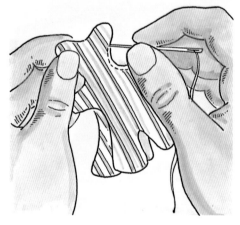

6 Cut out two matching pieces of fabric for the front and back of the bear. With cream sewing thread, sew the right sides together, leaving an opening at the top of the head. Turn inside out and fill with either potpourri or batting. Slipstitch opening in head. Trim neck with lace and flowers, and embroider eyes.

7 Sew a loop of blue ribbon to the bear with blue sewing thread.

8 When all sewing is complete, glue to the front of the card mount. Hang the bear from the central button at the top.

Clever Cat

~

Think of ways to personalize this card for a special event. For a child's birthday, you could use scraps from their favorite clothes, or do an appliqué picture of the family pet. For a mother's birthday — perhaps an appliqué picture of her favorite flowers, or a "portrait" of her home.

METHOD

1 Cut sixteen 2-inch squares from the printed fabrics and stitch together to form a block of four rows, with four squares in each row. Press.

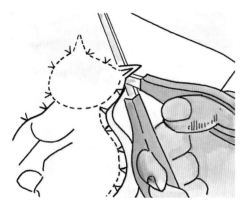

2 Transfer the cat template (see p125) and stitching lines to the muslin using dressmaker's carbon. Cut out, adding a ¼-inch seam allowance. Clip V-shapes of excess seam allowance and press under.

4 Carefully glue the patchwork to the front of the folded card. Stick a length of tape along each side to conceal the raw edges. This can be hand stitched or secured with a wide machine stitch in matching thread. Sew a button at each corner with brown embroidery thread and glue the patchwork to the card.

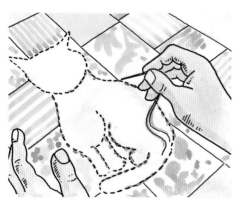

3 Slipstitch the cat to the patchwork square with white thread. With brown embroidery thread, sew a decorative small running stitch over the stitching lines. Sew the whiskers so that they overlap onto the patchwork, and work the nose in satin stitch. Work the eyes in green satin stitch. Press lightly.

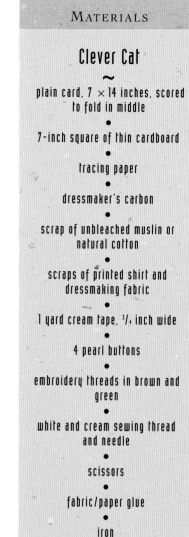

MATERIALS

Clever Cat

~

plain card, 7 × 14 inches, scored to fold in middle

•

7-inch square of thin cardboard

•

tracing paper

•

dressmaker's carbon

•

scrap of unbleached muslin or natural cotton

•

scraps of printed shirt and dressmaking fabric

•

1 yard cream tape, ¾ inch wide

•

4 pearl buttons

•

embroidery threads in brown and green

•

white and cream sewing thread and needle

•

scissors

•

fabric/paper glue

•

iron

Folk Art Angel

~

This angel could be made into a double-sided mobile or Christmas decoration by covering the reverse side to match the front and attaching a hanging loop of cord halfway along the back.

MATERIALS

Folk Art Angel

~

thin white cardboard,
6 × 12 inches

•

tracing paper

•

4 × 8-inch piece of printed cotton
fabric

•

3 × 7-inch piece of black felt

•

scrap of pale orange felt

•

iron-on fusible bonding

•

black felt-tip pen

•

scissors

•

iron

METHOD

1 Trace the angel template (see p124) on tracing paper, transferring all the markings. Trace the main silhouette on thin cardboard and cut out carefully.

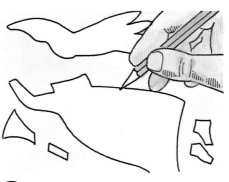

2 Reverse the tracing so that the angel now faces toward the left and trace the individual outlines for the dress, hair, shoes, and trumpet directly onto iron-on fusible bonding. Cut out each shape roughly.

3 Following the manufacturer's directions, iron the dress shape onto the reverse side of the printed fabric. Iron the hair and shoe patterns onto the black felt and the two sections of the trumpet onto the pale orange felt in the same way. Cut out all six pieces accurately around the pencil lines, and remove the backing papers.

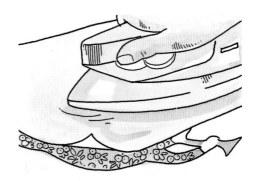

4 Place the dress shape on the angel cutout, carefully aligning the edges. Using a cloth to protect the surface, fuse in place with a cool iron. Attach the felt pieces in the same way, then draw in the eye with a fine felt-tip pen.

Cat with Tartan Ribbon

~

Interfacing has been used to make this cat, but you could use flocked paper, or flocking powder, available at craft shops.

METHOD

1 Glue a strip of the middle-sized ribbon across the card to form the wall.

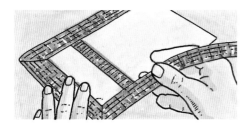

2 Glue a border of the widest tartan ribbon around the edges of the card, pleating it at the corners.

3 Draw and cut out a cat shape from the interfacing. If you use flocking powder, apply glue to a cat shape made from paper, sprinkle on the powder, and leave to dry.

4 Make two narrower bows from the ribbons. Glue the cat, bows, and beads to the card. Use beads for the cat's eye and nose.

Rabbit and Ribbons

~

Here is another way to use ribbons. This would make an attractive card for a new baby.

METHOD

1 Cut white board to approximately 4½ × 6 inches. Cut a window in center 2 × 3 inches.

2 Using glue or double-sided tape, attach decorative ribbon around edge of the white card.

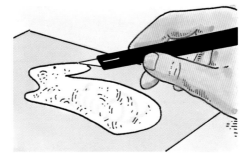

3 Cut rabbit shape from both blue board and batting. Place satin ribbon under cutout card with the batting rabbit beneath. Anchor with masking tape, sew nose and eye with black thread. Glue card rabbit to white mount.

4 Glue on tail. Glue eyelet lace around the edge of the ribbon.

5 Mount on blue board, and finally glue the pink bow in the top left-hand corner.

MATERIALS

Cat with Tartan Ribbon

~

plain card, 6¼ × 10¼ inches, scored to fold in middle

•

black interfacing or paper and flocking powder

•

bugle beads in different sizes

•

3 widths of tartan ribbon — ⅔, ⅓, ¼ inch

•

scissors

•

cutting mat

•

craft glue

Rabbit and Ribbons

~

blue and white poster board, 7 × 12¼ inches

•

batting

•

4 inches white satin ribbon, 1½ inches wide

•

30 inches decorative ribbon

•

1 yard white eyelet lace

•

1 pink satin bow

•

black thread

•

double-sided tape or craft glue

•

craft knife and cutting mat

MATERIALS

Homespun Star
~

plain card, 6 × 12 inches, scored
to fold in middle

•

6-inch squares of thin cardboard

•

tracing paper

•

scraps of different ginghams, and
red sewing thread

•

8-inch square of main fabric

•

scissors

•

masking tape

•

fabric/paper glue

Flower in Organza
~

plain blue card, 6 × 8¼ inches,
scored to fold in middle

•

pieces of pink silk and silk organza

•

small blue silk flower

•

fine silver thread

•

scissors

•

craft knife

•

cutting mat

•

fabric glue

•

iron-on adhesive (optional)

Homespun Star
~

*Made with scraps of gold and silver fabrics and
ribbons, this would also make an unusual
Christmas card.*

METHOD

1 Trace the star design from the template
(see page 124) and number each separate
piece. Using these as a guide, cut out five
triangles and one pentagon from gingham.

2 Cut out a circle 4 inches in diameter,
from a light-colored gingham. Glue the
pieces down onto it to form a star.

3 Glue the circle to the center of the
main fabric, and work a zigzag stitch by
hand or machine to cover the raw edges.
Stretch the finished piece over the square of
cardboard, folding the edges behind it, and
stick down with masking tape. Glue to the
front of the folded card.

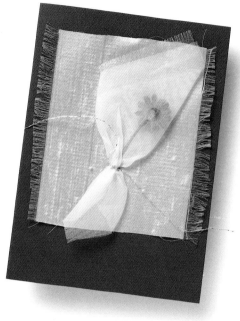

Flower in Organza
~

*For a special event, write a message on paper
and stain with diluted instant coffee so that it
looks like a scrap of parchment.*

METHOD

1 Cut a rectangle of silk to fit within the
front of the card. Ravel the silk on two
edges.

2 Cut a square of organza in proportion
to the size of the flower. Ravel the top edge.

3 Wrap the organza around the flower to
make a small "bouquet" (the flower should
point to one corner of the organza). Tie
with thread.

4 Glue the silk to the card, applying the
glue very thinly or it will stain the silk. As
an alternative, use iron-on adhesive.

5 Glue the bouquet to the silk, applying
glue only on the thread behind the bow –
again, do not glue this anywhere else or it
will stain the fabric.

Flower Print Vase
~

You will need one solid and two floral-print fabrics for this card. The flowers in one print should be separate enough to cut out, and the background color of this fabric should be the same as the solid fabric (in this case, muslin). The iron-on adhesive used to make the fabric adhere should also prevent it from fraying.

METHOD

1 Iron the two floral fabrics onto the adhesive, carefully following the manufacturer's directions.

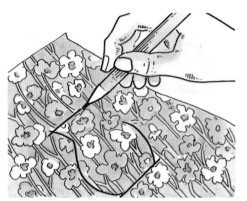

2 Draw a vase shape on the fabric with the smaller print, and cut out. Cut out single flowers from the other floral fabric.

4 Apply glue to the inside edge of the frame and lay it over the picture, making sure the fabric is stretched flat.

5 Glue the frame to the front of the card.

3 Remove the paper backing from the iron-on adhesive, and pin these shapes to the solid fabric background. Press with an iron, according to the manufacturer's directions. Measure around the vase and flowers, and from the card, cut a frame to fit around them.

MATERIALS

Flower Print Vase
~

plain card, 8¼ × 12½ inches, scored to fold in middle

•

card for frame, same size as front of folded card

•

fabric pen

•

2 floral-print fabrics

•

muslin, or other plain fabric

•

iron-on adhesive

•

scissors

•

ruler

•

craft knife

•

cutting mat

•

pins

•

fabric/paper glue

Gallery

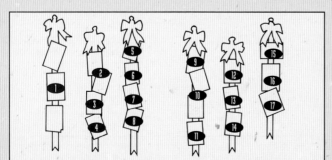

1 Whale/Heart/Crown
Tanya Marsh
Felt, fur fabric, and velvet appliquéd images are machine-appliquéd onto burlap. The inspiration for these cards came from an exhibition of African hand-appliquéd flags.

2 Tartan Heart/Tartan Flower
Thérèse McDermott
A pressed flower and a tartan heart are mounted on fabric and covered with printed acetate.

3 Pink Bouquet
Andrea Liss
Dried flowers, ribbons, lace, tissue paper, and a brass charm bow make up an intriguing 3-D card.

4 Gold Leaf Heart
Kate Twelvetrees
Silk with seed pearls is the background for a gold leaf heart wrapped in silk organza and tied with silver thread.

5 Tartan Tree
Sally Norris
Two tartan appliquéd fabrics form this jolly Christmas tree, which is machine stitched onto textured paper.

6 Country Bouquet
Andrea Liss
Layers of frayed fabric are the background for a simple bunch of dried flowers tied with satin ribbon.

7 **Silk Flowers**

Sophie Williams
Silk flowers are machine embroidered on silk.

8 **Golden Cherub**

Andrea Liss
Lace, fabric, and paper are the background for this foil cherub.

9 **Heart and Sole**

Ingrid Duffy
This card uses appliquéd patterned fabric, a stitched-on bead eye, and embroidery on a muslin background. The heart is painted on.

10 **Sunglasses Fish/Hearts and Flowers**

Jilly Marcuson
These hand-painted silk images use gold gutta in the same way as the card on page 101.

11 **Felt Flower**

Rebecca Salmon
This hand-stitched felt appliqué card uses simple color and outlines.

12 **African Man**

Susan Phrakhun
This machine-stitched collage with dried flowers and hand-printed figure is inspired by the primitive art of Africa.

13 **Magic Mirror**

Kate Twelvetrees
Four layers of frayed silk form a background for a tiny mirror.

14 **Flight to Freedom**

Kate Twelvetrees
Frayed silk and a gold net "cage" create the scene for the photocopied escaping bird, tinted with gold paint.

15 **Golden Crown**

Sophie Williams
A fake fur background holds a gold, machine-appliquéd crown with stitched color details.

16 **Wooly Sheep**

Ingrid Duffy
Denim, sheep's wool, and felt make up a touch-feely card! There is also an inked frame and title.

17 **Furry Piggy**

Cluck
Fake fur completely covers the back and the front of this card, except for the window revealing a drawn pig.

Abstract Silk Painting

~

Silk gives a special rich feeling to a card. The gutta used as a masking medium is like glue and stops the colors from running into each other.

MATERIALS

Abstract Silk Painting

~

plain card, 6¾ × 13½ inches, scored to fold in middle

•

cardboard for frame, same size as front of folded card

•

several pieces of paper, larger than the card

•

piece of silk, same size as front of card

•

different-colored silk dyes

•

gutta

•

medium-sized paintbrush

•

gutta dispenser (pen)

•

scissors

•

craft knife

•

cutting mat

•

ruler

•

pins or masking tape

•

craft glue

•

iron

METHOD

1 Cut a frame for your design from the framing card.

2 Draw your design on a piece of paper. Place silk fabric on top and pin or tape in place.

3 With the gutta dispenser, gently trace over the drawn lines. Allow the gutta to dry for 10–15 minutes.

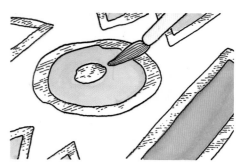

4 Dip the paintbrush into the dye. Slowly fill in the shapes by pressing the tip of the brush into the center of the area to be painted, and allowing the color to spread. Take care not to flood the silk. The gutta will keep the colors separate as long as there is not too much dye on the brush.

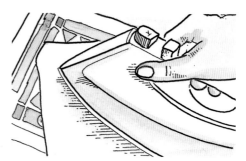

5 Allow the dye to dry. Cover design with a clean piece of paper and set the silk dye by holding an iron on the design according to the manufacturer's directions.

6 Wash the gutta out with cold water, and iron the design again between two sheets of clean paper.

7 Place the frame over the design and cut out the print. Spread glue along the inside edge of the frame. Lay it over the print, and glue to front of card, taking care not to get glue on silk.

Variation

This card has a simple cutout window, but for a special occasion try making a padded silk frame, using a cardboard base, batting, and a coordinating piece of solid-colored silk.

Silk Painted Card
~

The gutta acts as a barrier which helps to contain the colors, preventing one from bleeding into another. Usually the gutta is removed by washing, but in this case a gold metallic gutta has been used and has been left to form part of the design.

METHOD

1 Wash and dry silk and stretch it on the frame, using double-sided tape or map pins. Make sure it is very tightly stretched.

2 Using a pen, draw your design on the silk. (If you make a mistake, you can wash out the pen marks.) Alternately, draw the design on a piece of paper as in the method used for Abstract Silk Painting (opposite).

3 Using a continuous, strong line of gutta, go over the lines of your drawing, pressing and squeezing the tube at the same time to achieve this. Use the gutta to draw a border around the whole design.

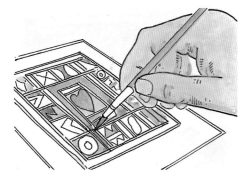

4 Prepare the colors according to the manufacturer's directions and paint the design using the tip of the paintbrush. The color will spread to the gutta edges, so there is no need to use heavy brushstrokes.

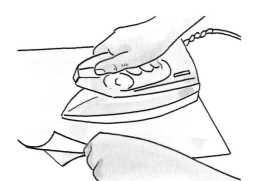

5 When the painting is complete, remove the design from the frame and iron it on the reverse side to set the colors, using a silk setting. Cover the design with cloth or paper and rotate the iron for about 5 minutes.

6 Cut the design out next to the gold gutta frame. This prevents fraying. Attach your design to the front of the card with double-sided tape or iron-on adhesive.

MATERIALS

Silk Painted Card
~

plain card, 6 × 8¼ inches, scored to fold in middle
•
medium-weight white silk
•
iron and cloth or paper for ironing
•
gold metallic gutta
•
silk paints
•
fabric pen
•
paintbrush
•
frame [from a craft shop, or use an old picture frame]
•
scissors
•
double-sided tape or map pins
•
iron-on adhesive

Glitter Bird

~

This card has been designed to hang up and is on a flat card rather than a folded one.

MATERIALS

Glitter Bird

~

poster board, 4¾ × 6 inches

•

colored paper for backing, 4¾ × 6 inches

•

tracing paper

•

scraps of silk fabric in four colors

•

feathers, sequins, "gems," beads, and decorative braid

•

fine gold thread

•

glitter braid, for edging

•

mixed-color glitter

•

iron-on adhesive

•

scissors

•

craft knife

•

cutting mat

•

craft glue

•

tape

METHOD

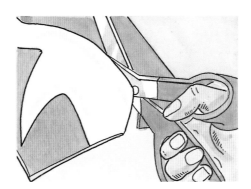

1 Iron a piece of silk fabric large enough for your bird onto the adhesive. Cut out the shape of the bird (you could draw the shape on paper first and lay it on the silk as a template).

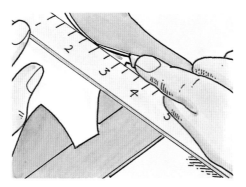

2 Lay the bird on the poster board and draw around it. Cut out a rectangle of board around the outline of the bird, but cut it just short of the beak and tail, so that these shapes project beyond the rectangle.

3 Cut out small pieces of silk for the wing and beak details and iron them on in the same way. Draw a line of glue around the edge of the bird with a fine point, and glue the gold thread to it to make an outline.

4 Apply glue to the rest of the board and sprinkle it with the glitter. Shake off the excess.

5 Use glue to attach all the feathers, beads, sequins, strips of braid, etc. Draw a line of glue around the edge of the card and glue on the glitter braid.

6 Use the tape to attach a loop of gold thread to the back of the card. Cover the back of the card with a piece of colored paper cut to the correct size. The finished card can be hung from the loop of gold thread.

Cross-stitched Heart

~

Try this design, embroidered in simple cross-stitch, for a card with an old-fashioned flavor.

METHOD

1 Using four strands of thread and following the diagram on p123, work the heart and bow on the Aida cloth in cross-stitch, making sure that all the stitches lie in the same direction. Press from the back.

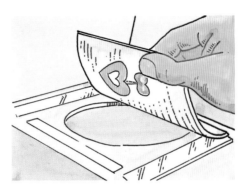

2 Stick lengths of double-sided tape around the back side of the card's oval opening. Cut the embroidery to size so that it is ¼ inch smaller on each side than the card. Peel the backing off the tape and carefully stick the Aida cloth face down in place, so that it is centered within the oval.

3 Fold the card flap over to cover the back of the embroidery and secure with more double-sided tape.

Variation
You could create a design of your own – perhaps an initial. Simply draw the outline on graph paper and fill in with pen each square which the line crosses. Use this as your pattern.

Felt Collage

~

Before you cut out the pieces for your collage, sketch a few designs on paper until you have created one you like. This card has been designed with a twenty-first birthday in mind.

METHOD

1 Cut out various shapes from felt using decorative and straight-edge scissors. You should have a larger piece for the background, and a variety of motifs to make up the design.

2 Arrange the pieces to achieve the best design. Glue the pieces in place.

3 Glue the finished collage to the front of the card.

MATERIALS

Felt Collage
~

- plain card made of textured paper, 7½ × 11 inches, scored to fold in middle
- scraps of felt in contrasting colors
- scissors
- pinking or other decorative-edge scissors
- craft glue

Cross-stitched Heart
~

- precut 3-fold card 6 × 8¼ inches, with oval window
- 4 × 6-inch rectangle of 14-count cream Aida cloth, or evenweave linen to fit behind oval of card
- stranded embroidery floss in dark green, rust, ocher, and gold
- needle
- scissors
- double-sided tape
- iron

For Your
Wedding

Introduction

Of course, all the cards in this book are a labor of love, but the cards in this section involve something a little extra or different. In some cases, such as the complex and delicate quilling cards, this is a meticulous new technique to learn and apply. Sometimes, the cards are evocative of another era. In other cases, what makes them extra special is the involvement of family or friends to create unique memories. These are particularly pleasing because the gifts of time and attention extend beyond the maker and the cards can be touching mementoes. Some of the cards have gifts to remove and use separately, and some are particularly unusual or decorative. One is in a highly decorated book form, and

another is not, strictly speaking, a card at all. The very best thing about making your own cards is that they can be totally unique, completely personal both to the giver and recipient. Explore this avenue of possibilities with your imagination.

Labor of Love

Ribbon Rose Bouquet
~

Make this romantic bouquet from a few lengths of ribbon, a small piece of silk, and some decorative lace edging.

METHOD

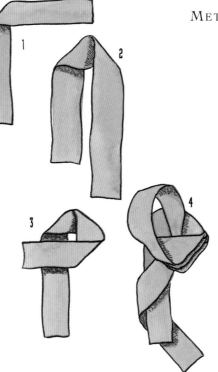

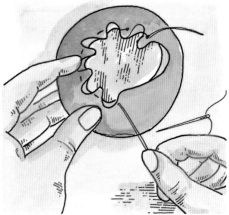

1 Make several ribbon roses in different colors and widths, reserving narrow and green ribbons for Step 4. To do this, fold the ribbon at a right angle, two-thirds along its length, then fold as in the illustration above. When you reach the end of your ribbon, use your fingers to open out the center of your rose into a rounded flower. Make several stab stitches through the base of the rose to hold the ribbon in place.

2 Cut a circle of batting the same size as the cardboard circle, and glue them together. Gather the edge of the pink silk or satin circle to fit over the padded circle and slipstitch in place.

3 Neatly join the two ends of the lace, and gather to fit the circle. Sew in place, adjusting the folds.

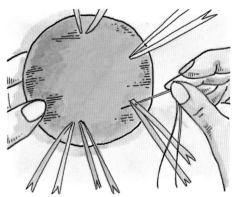

4 Sew a few streamers of narrow ribbon to the padded circle. Then sew or glue on loops of green ribbon "leaves," and the ribbon roses.

5 Use fabric glue to mount the bouquet on the front of the card.

Wedding Veil

~

*Write a "secret" message under the lace, before
tying the handkerchief to the card, to be
discovered when the handkerchief is removed.*

METHOD

1 Cut heart shapes from thin cardboard.
Apply a thin layer of glue to one side and
press the hearts onto the gold leaf. Leave to
dry, and then lift them off carefully. The
gold leaf will have adhered to the hearts,
with loose pieces around the edges: fold
these behind the hearts. Alternatively, paint
the hearts gold.

2 Cover the card rectangle with the
paper, folding it over the edges and gluing
behind the card.

3 Gather the handkerchief together near
the top and, holding it between your
fingers, position it on the card. Mark the
card on each side of the gathering, close to
the fabric.

4 Remove the handkerchief and make
small holes at the points marked. Thread
the ribbon through the holes from the back
and tie around the handkerchief, making a
bow. Allow plenty of ribbon so that the
hanging ends are long.

5 Glue the hearts to the rectangle, and
the rectangle to the front of the card.

Paper Lace Valentine

~

*Printed scraps were used by Victorians to
decorate screens and for many other purposes —
a technique known as "decoupage."*

METHOD

1 Cut a rectangular shape from a white
paper doily. Cut out individual motifs such
as hearts or flowers from the other doilies,
looking for interesting shapes.

2 Draw around the outside of the doily
shape on the colored paper, marking where
some of the holes in the "lace" are. Cut out
the colored paper and glue the doily to the
paper shape.

3 Glue the doily to the card to leave a
small border all the way around.

4 Use your imagination to decorate the
card in elaborate Victorian style with cutout scraps and motifs from the other doilies.
Gold and silver foil are especially effective.

MATERIALS

Wedding Veil
~
plain cream card, 6¾ × 12 inches,
scored to fold in middle
•
thin cardboard for hearts
•
rectangle of thin cardboard same
size as the front of card
•
decorative background paper
•
handkerchief, as lacy as possible
•
thin blue ribbon
•
mock gold leaf transfer sheet, or
gold paint
•
scissors
•
fabric/paper glue

Paper Lace Valentine
~
colored plain card, 8¼ × 12½ inches,
scored and folded in middle
•
colored paper for backing doily
•
paper doilies in white, gold, and
silver
•
reproduction Victorian scraps
•
sharp scissors
•
craft knife
•
cutting mat
•
paper glue

Ribbon Frame Card
~

MATERIALS

Ribbon Frame Card
~

plain card, 7 × 10¼ inches, made from thick watercolor paper with a deckle edge, scored to fold in middle

•

clip frame, same size as front of card (optional)

•

backing fabric, slightly smaller than front of card

•

black-and-white family photograph, or a laser copy reduced to suitable size

•

4 small dried roses or silk flowers

•

narrow ribbon, approximately ½ inch wide, to frame the photograph and cross over (or braid three lengths of narrow ribbon)

•

scissors

•

fabric/paper glue

You could buy a clip frame and a greeting card box from a craft shop, make the mount to fit the frame, and send the card and frame together. The roses on this card are not attached to the ribbon, so they can be easily removed, tucked into the clip frame, glued to the glass, or hung from the frame with ribbon. To make the deckle edge of the card, rip the edge along a ruler, or use craft scissors designed for this purpose. When gluing on the ribbon, avoid using too much glue or it will stain the ribbon. Choose a good fabric glue that will allow you to rub off the excess when dry.

METHOD

1 Glue the backing fabric to the card, then glue the photo in place on top of the fabric.

2 Apply a thin line of glue running from the center of the bottom edge of the photo to one bottom corner. Lay the ribbon on this with a loose end of ribbon at the center bottom of the photo. Wait a few minutes until it is dry.

3 Apply a line of glue along the adjacent vertical edge of the photo. Turn the ribbon and lay it along this line of glue, leaving a small pleat of ribbon at the corner of the photo. Again, wait until dry.

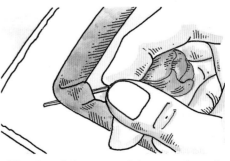

4 Glue the ribbon along the remaining two and a half sides of the photo in the same way, leaving a small open pleat at each corner and a second loose end in the center bottom edge of the photograph.

5 Cross over the ends of the ribbon at the bottom center and glue down the ends. If you are using narrow satin ribbon, make it into a bow.

6 Thread the stems of the roses through the open pleats in the corners.

Family Flowers

~

This card can be used for a variety of special occasions – for an anniversary, a thank-you card from a family, a bon-voyage card from a group of friends, or a really large bouquet of mixed flowers for a great-grandparent's birthday. For this card, flat, open flowers with large centers work best.

METHOD

MATERIALS

Family Flowers

~

cream card for mount,
9½ × 9½ inches, scored and folded
in center

•

colored paper for background, same
size as front of card

•

small cutout faces from
photographs to fit flower centers

•

silk flowers

•

wide ribbon in organza or similar
fabric

•

scissors

•

craft knife

•

cutting mat

•

craft glue

1 Remove the flower heads from the stems and cut off any remaining stem as close to the back of the flower head as possible. Glue the flower heads to the background paper and glue the photographs to the flower centers.

4 Lay the picture on the cream card and mark it so you have a narrow border. Carefully mount the picture, applying glue to the card rather than the picture itself.

2 Cut the stems an appropriate length and arrange them under the edges of the flowers to look as though they come from the flower centers.

3 Lay a long piece of ribbon across the card and attach the center to the card with a dab of glue. Glue the stems in place over the ribbon. When dry, tie the ribbon around the stems in a bow.

Autographed Hearts
~

Break the wax seal to reveal the messages in this heart-shaped book. This is an ideal card to send from several members of a group – a colleague's retirement card, for instance.

MATERIALS

Autographed Hearts
~

plain card, 5¼ × 5¼ inches
•
thin blue cardboard,
10½ × 10½ inches
•
typing paper for hearts
•
silver thread
•
rubber stamp and inkpad
•
rubber stamp and embossing kit
(optional)
•
red sealing wax, taper, and bowl of
water
•
needle and thread
•
decorative-edge scissors
•
fabric/paper glue

METHOD

1 Fold the blue cardboard in half and draw a heart so that the top touches the fold. Using decorative-edge scissors, cut the two hearts out through the two layers, so that they are still joined at the top.

2 Cut out hearts from the typing paper in the same way and the same size as those from the blue cardboard – each cut makes two pages, so the number you cut out depends on the number of hearts you want in the book.

3 Lay the folded paper hearts inside the heart-shaped cover and stitch the sheets to the cover where the hearts join at the top. If you do this very slightly behind the fold, you will not be able to see the stitches from the front. The paper hearts need not be registered exactly under the cover, as any visible edges will make an interesting effect. Make a small hole near the bottom of the heart cover, pass the silver thread through, and make a loop.

4 If you wish, you can decorate the cover and inside pages with a rubber stamp. The hearts on this card have been embossed using an embossing kit (see page 45). Glue the heart notebook to the card.

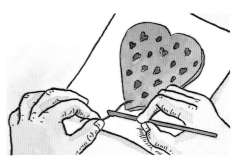

5 After everyone has filled in a page of the card, mask the card with spare paper. Stand a taper in a jar and cover your work surface. Light the taper. Hold the thread and heart with one hand so that the thread is stretched taut on the card and to one side of the heart. Hold the stick of sealing wax in the other hand and heat the end in the flame. As soon as the wax begins to soften – this happens very quickly – press the end of the stick onto the loop. You may have to do this several times. Hold the loop stretched until the sealing wax is dry (about 30 seconds).

6 Make small holes and attach a loop of thread to the top of the card, so that it can be hung up, or make a stand at the back (see Stand-up Goose on page 68).

Safety Warning
Be very careful with sealing wax – it gets extremely hot. Take care that the stick of wax does not flare up in the taper flame and have a bowl of water ready to dip it into if necessary. When you buy sealing wax, follow the manufacturer's directions.

Victorian Silk Heart
~

This card is in the style of a Victorian Valentine and uses lace, scraps, and padding for the heart. See also Paper Lace Valentine, page 107.

METHOD

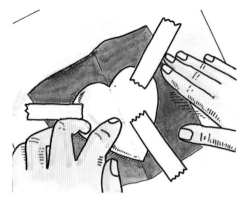

1 Mark and then cut out a heart-shaped window from the center of the black card. Cut a similar heart shape from the batting. Lay the piece of satin over the batting, and push the satin and batting gently through the heart window to create a padded effect. Tape this securely in place behind the card.

4 Glue two pink ribbon bows above and below the heart.

5 Turn the card over and stick a strip of double-sided tape right around the edge. Stick lengths of lace to it so that they form a frame around the card. Glue the ends of the lace together.

6 Finally, glue the whole design to the front of the card.

2 Cut out the picture scraps and arrange them around the heart, to the edge of the black card. Allow some to overlap the others. Glue in place.

3 Cut a length of pink ribbon and a length of lace. Glue the ribbon to the card below the heart, pleating it at the point. Glue the lace on top in the same way, allowing some of the ribbon to show. Cover the ends with two picture scraps.

MATERIALS

Victorian Silk Heart
~

plain dark red card, 8 × 14 inches, scored to fold in middle of long side

•

rectangle of black cardboard approximately ¼ inch smaller all around than front of card

•

2 sheets Victorian reproduction scraps (available from stationers or by mail order)

•

1 yard cream lace

•

2 purchased pink satin bows (or make them with thin satin ribbon)

•

cream satin ribbon approximately 3 × 3 inches

•

1 yard pink ribbon

•

batting

•

scissors

•

double-sided tape

•

craft glue

Corrugated Book Card
~

Look for a variation of these fascinating cards in the gallery section. Uniquely, the four sides of this card are embellished with different but complementary designs. Use the ideas as a wonderful source of inspiration.

METHOD

Front of card

1 Peel the top layer off the corrugated cardboard so that you can decorate the more interesting textured surface beneath. Punch two holes in each of the corrugated pieces of cardboard.

2 Use fray-check on the sides of the tapestry fabric to prevent fraying, following the manufacturer's directions. Glue to the middle front of the card. Place the postcard on the fabric and glue. Weight with a heavy book to dry flat.

3 Decorate the card by adding on grass, dried flowers, a tassel, and decorative buttons or charms. Reinforce with a few stitches where necessary, using invisible thread.

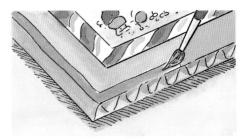

4 Cover all threads and holes on the rear front by gluing on gift-wrap paper. Paint the edges of the card front with gold leaf paint.

Inside and back of card

5 Cover the greeting page with hand-made paper and textured paper. Use an appropriate rubber stamp for your greeting.

6 Turn the card over and stencil a design on the card using acrylic or stencil paints. When dry, glue on pearls, in accordance with the design.

Assembly

7 Cut 2 strips of suede and ribbon approximately ⅛ × 11 inches. Place the front and back of the card together and thread the strips through the holes, tying loosely, so that the card can easily be opened.

Collected Letters
~

This card was inspired by friendship quilts, in which each square is made by friends or family and then joined together. For a special birthday or other occasion, prepare well in advance. Ask friends or family to help you make a card which contains their thoughts and memories of the recipient, and which can be treasured for many years.

METHOD

1 Cut or tear small pieces of watercolor paper, each about 3 × 3½ inches. Tearing gives a more attractive edge: to do this, fold paper sharply and tear along a straightedge or ruler. Send one sheet to each of the friends or family you would like to contribute to the card. Ask them to write a message, make a drawing, copy a poem, include pressed flowers, or leaves, seeds, or photographs – anything that reminds them of the person who will receive the card. Both sides of the paper can be used, but no objects should be bigger than one-fourth of the paper size.

2 When you receive the "letters" back, fold them in four and wrap in tissue paper, including any flowers, etc. Writing looks interesting when parts of it are seen through the paper. Do not glue the packages – simply fold the paper at the back.

3 Place the packages on the background paper, then cut it to size with decorative-edge scissors; if you don't have these, tear as described in Step 1. Make small holes in the background with a pin at center top and bottom of each package, as close to the package as possible – you can mark the points in pencil first.

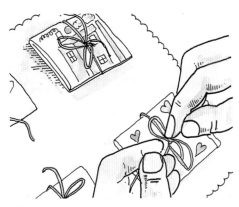

4 Push lengths of the gold thread through the holes from the back of the paper and tie the packages to the background using double bows.

5 Glue the backing paper to the card. The messages can be unwrapped and read, but because the thread is glued to the card under the backing paper, it will not slip out through the holes and the letters can be wrapped again and tied back onto the card to keep.

MATERIALS

Collected Letters
~
plain card,
8½ × 13 inches, scored to fold
along top center
•
thick paper or thin cardboard for
background
•
textured watercolor paper
•
white tissue paper
•
gold thread
•
decorative-edge scissors
•
craft knife
•
cutting mat
•
pin
•
fabric/paper glue
•
pencil

Gallery

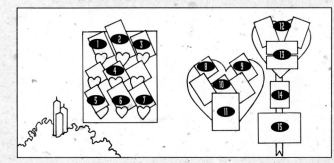

1 Key to my Heart
Kate Twelvetrees
An embossed copper heart is wrapped in silk organza, tied with gold thread, then mounted on frayed silk with a hanging, wrapped antique key.

2 Butterflies
Wendy Beardmore
In an even more painstaking variation of the card on page 109, each layer of the butterfly's wings is added separately with a toothpick.

3 Carnation
Jane Lord
This handmade paper uses real carnation petals, giving a very delicate effect.

4 Peacock/Running Hare/Birds Laying Egg
Julie Morgan
The images on these cards are drawn on textured backgrounds and then combined with collaged, handmade, and painted papers.

5 Heart through a Window
Personal Stamp Exchange
A padded heart within a stamped, embossed decorative border is glimpsed through a cutout beribboned window.

6 Autumn Leaves
Personal Stamp Exchange
Soft torn tissue-paper edges and colors reflect the embossed, stamped autumn leaves, edged with a twig bound with thin gold wire.

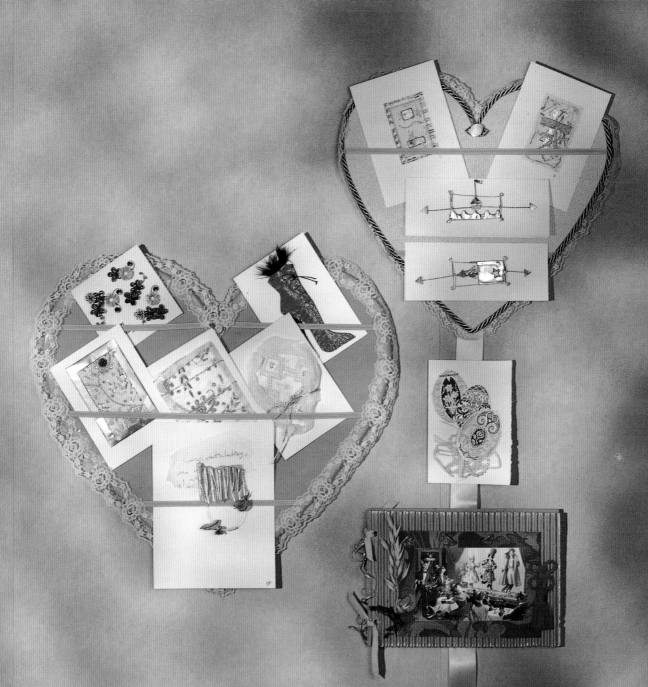

Potpourri Keepsake
~

This card is sealed with ribbon which can be retied after the message has been read. It could then be kept to scent a drawer. You could include a verse from a favorite poem, or write a letter or message using calligraphy to make it more decorative. For a special occasion, perhaps include a small gift such as a scented lace handkerchief, inside the card.

Potpourri Keepsake
~

thick watercolor paper mat, 7 × 11 inches, scored to fold along the top and with deckle edges

•

smaller rectangle of the same paper

•

pretty handmade paper or deckle-edged paper, diluted coffee, and gold paint (optional — see Step 3)

•

potpourri or dried lavender mixed with dried rose petals

•

dried rosebud

•

fine lace fabric

•

narrow satin ribbon to match roses

•

rubber stamp or stencil (optional — see Step 5)

•

fabric/paper glue

METHOD

1 Place dried rose petals on the rectangle of paper and cover with lace. Turn the paper and lace over carefully and glue the edges behind, forming a "present." Alternately, use the decorative selvage of the lace at the top, in which case don't fold and glue the top edge, but stitch through it with white thread to enclose the petals. Tie the "present" with ribbon, knotting behind.

2 Pierce two holes at the bottom corners of the mat, through both layers. Pass a long piece of ribbon through these holes from the back of the card. Make sure the two ends of ribbon coming through to the front of the card are equal in length. Tie a knot in each of these ends about 3 inches from the edge of the mount.

3 Write a letter or message on pretty paper and glue it inside the card. Alternately, if you are using a verse, write it on a piece of deckle-edged paper, then stain the paper with diluted coffee to "antique" it, tint with gold paint, and glue it inside the card.

4 After writing the message inside the card, wrap the ribbon back around the edges and tie with a bow in the center back of the card. The card will stand up after it has been opened, but because the ribbon can't slip out, the card can be resealed.

5 Finally, glue the potpourri "present" to the front of the card, and perhaps decorate the back with a rubber stamped or stenciled pattern. Tuck a dried rosebud behind the ribbon.

Cassette Wedding Card
~

Messages of goodwill from the family, a tape of romantic music, or something amusing – this is a novelty wedding card that would be fun to make with the children of the family.

METHOD

1 Wrap the cassette box in silver tissue and tie with silver ribbon. Attach to the center of the mount with the self-adhesive pad.

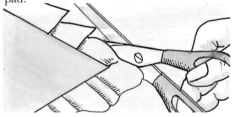

2 Cut strips of silver tissue paper, pleat, and glue around the edge. When dry, cut a wavy pattern along the edges.

3 Apply a wavy line of glue just inside the edge of the mount. Sprinkle with silver glitter and shake off the excess.

4 Cut two small dove shapes from silver card and make holes for their eyes. Decorate the edges with glitter as before.

5 Wrap cake decoration flowers in tissue and tie with ribbon. Glue on bouquets, doves, and other cake decorations.

Driftwood Greeting
~

For a completely different type of greeting, experiment with sending your message on other materials, such as this simple piece of driftwood.

METHOD

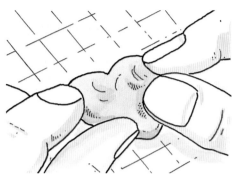

1 Make a small heart from clay – either quite flat like a drop of liquid metal, or rounded, as if padded, according to taste. Paint it with glue to seal. If using polymer clay, follow manufacturer's directions carefully.

2 When dry, paint the heart gold. When the paint has dried completely, glue the heart to the driftwood.

3 Tear a piece of paper to the same shape as the back of the driftwood. Write your message on the paper, and bind it to the wood using the gold thread. Alternatively, you can tear a thin strip of paper to fit around the wood, write your message all the way along it, and then anchor it around the wood with double-sided tape.

back

front

MATERIALS

Cassette Wedding Card
~

plain card, 6¼ × 8 inches
•
silver card
•
silver tissue
•
cassette tape
•
silver cake decorations, including flowers
•
silver glitter
•
silver ribbon in two widths
•
scissors
•
craft knife
•
cutting mat
•
self-adhesive pad
•
craft glue

Driftwood Greeting
~

piece of handmade textured paper
•
modelling clay or polymer
•
small piece of driftwood
•
gold thread
•
gold acrylic paint
•
double-sided tape [optional – see Step 3]
•
craft glue

Take my Heart
~

The list of instructions for this card are only a guide. Experiment with different ways of making hearts, other bought or found objects, wider threads and ribbons, and different-colored mats. To achieve the deckled edge on the watercolor, tear it along a sharp edge, such as a metal ruler, or use decorative-edge scissors.

MATERIALS

Take my Heart
~
cream-colored plain card, 4½ × 12 inches, scored to fold in middle
•
watercolor paper, torn to size (see page 13)
•
white tissue paper
•
thin copper sheet
•
purchased "gold" heart
•
brooch finding
•
gold cord
•
fine gold thread
•
gold and pink acrylic paint
•
sharp scissors
•
metal file
•
craft glue
•
all-purpose glue

METHOD

1 Cut tiny hearts and a larger one for the brooch from the copper (sharp scissors are fine), and file all the edges smooth.

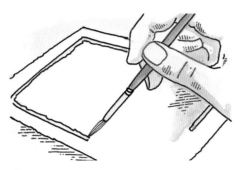

2 Dab or paint small areas of the watercolor paper with gold and pink paint, or paint a "frame" of gold. Tie the paper like a present with gold cord, gluing the ends in place just under the edges of the paper.

3 Suspend the bought heart with fine thread from the top of the paper and glue on the tiny hearts.

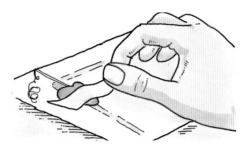

4 Tear tiny strips of tissue. Apply craft glue to these, either with the fingers or a brush, and pleat and stretch them over all the hearts and some parts of the cord. When dry, brush quite dry gold paint over the creases in the tissue to make it look like fine gold cloth. (The tissue stretched over the jewelry heart binds it to the paper and gives it a more interesting finish.) Glue the paper to the card.

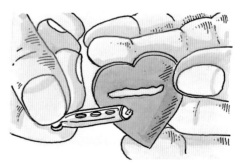

5 Stretch pleated tissue with craft glue over the larger copper heart, wrap it behind, and leave to dry. Highlight the tissue pleats with gold paint. Using all-purpose glue, attach the brooch finding to the back of the heart. When it is really dry, pin the brooch over the cord on the card.

Silver Dove Decoration

~

You can buy thin sheet aluminum or use metallic card or cardboard painted gold or silver. The soft handmade paper used for the background gives an interesting edge when it is torn.

METHOD

1 Draw or trace the shape for the decoration – star, crown, dove, etc. Cut this from the aluminum using scissors. Also cut out two small stars and file all edges smooth.

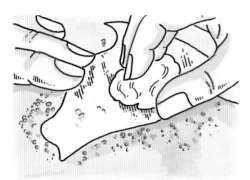

2 Sprinkle some sand on a work surface and lay the decoration on top. Rub the decoration with paper towels or cotton, pressing it against the grains of sand to achieve an embossed effect. Emboss lines on the backs of the small stars. Using the point of a used ballpoint pen, emboss a raised spot for the bird's eye.

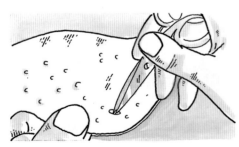

3 Make a small hole at the top of the bird. Thread silver thread through this, and tie it in a loop.

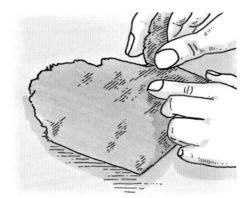

4 Tear an egg-like shape from the blue paper and glue this to the card. Fingerprint or stipple gold paint on the blue background. Attach the two small stars to the paper with double-sided tape.

5 Finally hang the decoration over the front of the card and fix it inside the card, using magic tape so that it can be removed easily for future use.

MATERIALS

Silver Dove Decoration

~

plain card, 5¼ × 8½ inches, scored to fold in middle

•

soft, dark blue handmade paper

•

paper towels or piece of absorbent cotton

•

sheet aluminum

•

sand

•

silver thread

•

gold acrylic paint

•

used ballpoint pen

•

double-sided tape

•

magic tape

•

scissors

•

metal file

•

cutting mat

•

fabric/paper glue

Basic Quilling
~

For quilling you can use either a needle tool or a slotted tool. The needle tool makes a smaller center in the rolls and so makes a more attractive design. The slotted tool is easier to use because the slot catches and holds the paper, but it leaves a bend in the paper. The weight of quilling paper is most important; it rolls smoothly, opens evenly, and holds its shape well. The standard width paper is ⅛ inch. Make the board by wrapping waxed paper around a piece of corrugated cardboard.

OTHER MATERIALS

quilling board [see right]
•
tweezers
•
straight pins
•
ruler
•
scissors
•
clear-drying craft glue

Quilling: To practice, tear off a strip of quilling paper of the length specified in the instructions. To roll with the needle tool, slightly moisten one end of the paper and place that end against the end of your index finger. Position the quilling tool on the end of the paper and press the paper around the tool with your thumb. Roll the paper around the tool with your thumb, keeping the edges as even as possible. Remove the paper from the tool and glue the loose end. When you are first learning, roll each strip in the center of the needle. After you have become proficient, you may want to use the needle's tip instead. It will leave a smaller hole in the roll's center.

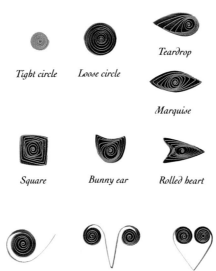

Tight circle   *Loose circle*

Teardrop

Marquise

Square   *Bunny ear*   *Rolled heart*

Loose scroll   *Open heart*   *V scroll*

Quilling shapes: The following rolls and scrolls are used in these two designs.
Tight circle: Roll, slide the roll off the tool, and glue the loose end closed.
Loose circle: Roll. Slide off tool and allow the coils to expand. Glue the loose end.
Teardrop: Roll a loose circle and pinch a point on one side.
Marquise: Roll a loose circle and pinch on opposite sides.
Square: Make a marquise. Turn it 90 degrees and pinch it again.
Bunny ear: Roll a loose circle. Make a rounded indentation on one side.
Rolled heart: Make a loose circle. Pinch a point on one side. Then make a sharp indentation on the opposite side. Be sure all three points are very sharp.
Loose scroll: Roll one end of the strip, leaving the other end loose.
Open heart: Crease a length of paper in the center. Roll each end in toward the crease.
V scroll: Crease a length of paper at its center. Roll each end toward the outside.

METHOD

1 Draw your pattern on a separate piece of paper. Roll the quilling paper with the slotted tool by threading paper into the slot of the tool. Slide the tool to near the strip's end and turn it in a circular motion, keeping the edges even.

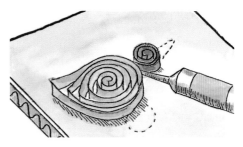

2 Slip your pattern under the waxed paper on the quilling board and pin the first roll directly over the pattern. Use a small amount of glue to attach the second roll to the first.

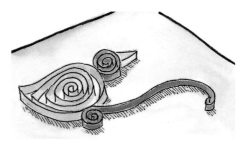

3 Continue adding rolls, using pins to secure them until the glue is dry, as needed. Remove the pins and gently lift the design from the waxed paper. Attach to background with glue, as in the designs shown.

Welcome to the World
~

Balloons: Three 12-inch teardrops, three 3-inch rolled hearts for knots, and three short lengths of paper for string.

Ball: Glue a deep blue 24-inch length, a pale pink 12-inch length, and a 12-inch deep blue length together end to end. Roll into a tight circle beginning with the deep blue 24-inch length. Gently push the center out to make a conical roll and then spread a thin layer of glue on the inner surface to help it retain its shape.

Sailboat: 8-inch irregular shape (for hull), five 2-inch tight circles for mast, sail cut from white paper.

Kite: Background diamond cut from deep blue paper, 3-inch white open heart glued into an 3½-inch V scroll; 4-inch white open heart glued into a 4½-inch V scroll; six 2-inch colored teardrops; short length of white paper across width of kite; short length of deep blue paper for the tail.

Teddy bear: 24-inch loose circle (body), two 3-inch teardrops (arms), two 6-inch loose circles (feet), 12-inch loose circle (head), two 2-inch bunny ears (ears), two 1-inch tight circles (eyes), 2-inch tight circle (nose). Add a small yellow bow.

Blocks: Use ¼-inch-wide paper to make three 3-inch red, yellow, and blue squares. Print a letter on each square.

Duck: 15-inch shaped yellow teardrop for body, 3-inch loose circle for head, two 3-inch tight circles for feet; length of beige paper for making triangular beak, and string.

Quilled Wedding Card
~

Butterfly: Cut a 1 × 4-inch triangle and roll into a bead beginning with the wide end of triangle. Each wing is a 6-inch and a 4-inch teardrop (standard width) glued together. Wrap a length of gold quill trim around each teardrop.

Flowers: Make four soft ivory flowers using 4-inch bunny ears, two flowers using 3-inch bunny ears, and three flowers using 2-inch bunny ears.

Flower centers: Glue soft ivory to soft green and roll into a tight circle beginning the roll with the soft ivory. For each large flower, use 2½-inch soft ivory and ½-inch soft green. The medium flowers use 2 inches of soft ivory and ½ inch of soft green, the small flowers use 1½ inches soft ivory and ½ inch of soft green.

Leaves: Cut six leaves from ⅜ inch wide green paper and six leaves from ⅜ inch wide gold quill trim.

Scrolls: 1-inch and 2-inch pale green loose scrolls.

Templates
~

All of the templates shown on pages 122–125 are actual size. You can simply photocopy them from the book and cut out the copy. If you do not have access to a photocopier, make your own copy using tracing paper.

Homespun Star

page 96

Folk Art Angel

page 94

Stenciled Hearts

page 58

Clever Cat
page 93

Stencil Sunface
page 60

Silkscreen Print
page 50

Hand and Heart

page 38

Classic Vase

page 63

Stand-up Goose

page 68

Templates
~

Cross-stitched Heart
page 103

3-D Star
page 69
Reduced by 50 per cent

Stand-up Pig
page 69

Index

Card Makers

~

Quarto would like to thank all the cardmakers who have kindly allowed us to include their cards in this book.

Special thanks to the following agents for their help and interest: **Elka de Wit** at The Elk, 67 Brighton Road, London N16 8EQ (tel. (171) 249 9181), representing cardmakers **Thérèse McDermott, Julie Morgan, Judy Pickering,** and **Alana Pryce;** and **Jain Suckling** at **Funky Eclectica,** 12 First Avenue, London W10 4NL (tel. (181) 964 9411), representing **Irene Baron, Judy Caplin, Cluck, Susan Codmer, Jan Cooper, Julie Dean, Ingrid**

Duffy, Hand and Heart Design, Susan Luqman, Mayhem Designs, Rosalind Miller, Helen rowan, Sands, Penny Saxby, Sparkle Designs and Sophie Williams. **Kate Twelvetrees'** cards are distributed in the US by **The English Card Company** (tel. (516) 627 3011), or she can be contacted at her London studio on (181) 809 1593. **Vinci Draper** at **The English Card Company,** 14c Hargrave Park, London N19 5JL, also distributes cards by **Sarah Jane Brown, Jilly Marcuson,** and **Sally Norris.**
Andrea Liss can be contacted at **Hannah Handmade Cards,** Evanston, Illinois; **Malinda**

Johnston is at the L:ake City Craft Co, Nixa, Montana. **The Crescent Cardboard Company** are based in Wheeling, Illinois; Paper Troupe are in Bensenville, Illinois; and the **Personal Stamp Exchange** are in Petaluma, California.

All other cardmakers can be contacted care of Quarto Publishing.

Quarto would also like to thank Amazing Grates, 61–63 High Road, London N2 8AB for supplying mantelpieces for photography.

Project Makers

~

Kate Twelvetrees 20, 24, 25, 26, 27 (right), 28, 29, 30, 31, 36, 40, 41, 49, 51, 53 (left), 56 (right), 57, 73 (right), 96 (right), 107 (left), 108, 109, 110, 113, 116, 117 (right), 118, 119
Lucinda Ganderton 38, 39 (left and right), 60 (right), 68, 88, 93, 94, 96 (left), 103 (right), 106, 107 (right)
Fenella Brown 21 (left), 23, 34, 46, 62, 63, 72, 89, 90, 91, 92, 95 (left and right), 97, 100, 102, 111, 117 (left)
Mary Fellows 21 (right), 22, 35, 47, 48, 58, 59

Elaine Hill 27 (left), 53 (right), 60 (left), 61, 66, 67, 69 (right), 81, 84
Melanie Brasch 69 (left), 70, 71, 73 (left), 76, 77, 78, 79, 83 (left and right), 85, 103 (left)
Clare Baggaley and Sally Bond 82
Cari Haysom 52, 56 (left), 57 (left)
Bobbie Hamburg 112
Tushar Parekh 37 (left and right)
Rachel Purser 80
Malinda Johnstone 120, 121
Michelle Powell 44, 45
Sarbjit Natt 50, 101